WORKBOOK

Focus on GRAMMAR 3B

FOURTH EDITION

WORKBOOK

Focus on
GRAMMAR 3B

FOURTH EDITION

Marjorie Fuchs

ALWAYS LEARNING

PEARSON

Focus on Grammar 3B: An Integrated Skills Approach, Fourth Edition Workbook

Copyright © 2012, 2006, 2000, 1995 by Pearson Education, Inc.
All rights reserved.

Pearson Education, Inc., 10 Bank Street, White Plains, NY 10606

Staff credits: The people who made up the *Focus on Grammar 3B, Fourth Edition, Workbook* team, representing editorial, production, design, and manufacturing, are: Aerin Csigay, Christine Edmonds, Nancy Flaggman, Ann France, Stacey Hunter, Lise Minovitz, and Robert Ruvo.

Cover image: Shutterstock.com
Text composition: ElectraGraphics, Inc.
Text font: New Aster

Photo credits: **Page 101** Shutterstock.com; **p. 102** Shutterstock.com; **p. 109** Images Source/Getty Images; **p. 120** Shutterstock.com; **p. 125** Colin Garratt/Milepost 92½/ Corbis; **p. 128** Shutterstock.com; **p. 142** RubberBall Productions; **p. 147** (all) Shutterstock.com; **p. 166** Shutterstock.com

Illustrations: **ElectraGraphics, Inc.:** pp. 108, 131–132, 136, 153, 169, 171–172, 179; **Susan Scott:** pp. 199, 190

ISBN 10: 0-13-217044-2
ISBN 13: 978-0-13-217044-4

Printed in the United States of America

6 7 8 9 10   V092   16 15 14 13

CONTENTS

ABOUT THE AUTHOR

Marjorie Fuchs has taught ESL at New York City Technical College and LaGuardia Community College of the City University of New York and EFL at the Sprach Studio Lingua Nova in Munich, Germany. She has a master's degree in Applied English Linguistics and a Certificate in TESOL from the University of Wisconsin—Madison. She has authored and co-authored many widely used books and multimedia materials, notably *Crossroads, Top Twenty ESL Word Games: Beginning Vocabulary Development, Families: Ten Card Games for Language Learners, Focus on Grammar 4: An Integrated Skills Approach, Focus on Grammar 3 CD-ROM, Focus on Grammar 4 CD-ROM, Longman English Interactive 3* and *4, Grammar Express Basic, Grammar Express Basic CD-ROM, Grammar Express Intermediate, Future 1: English for Results,* and workbooks for *The Oxford Picture Dictionary High Beginning* and *Low Intermediate, Focus on Grammar 3* and *4,* and *Grammar Express Basic.*

UNIT 17 Nouns and Quantifiers

EXERCISE 1: Nouns

A. *Read the article about an ancient Egyptian king. Underline the nouns.*

TUT'S TOMB[1]: AN EGYPTIAN TIME CAPSULE

Tutankhamun, better known as King Tut, became king of ancient Egypt when he was only nine years old. He died before his nineteenth birthday around 1323 B.C.E., and was mostly forgotten. Thousands of years later, British archeologist Howard Carter searched for his tomb. In 1922, after searching for many years, he finally found it near the Nile River, across from the modern Egyptian city of Luxor. Inside he discovered thousands of items buried along with the young king. Among the many treasures[2] were:

- furniture—including couches and chairs
- jewelry—including bracelets and necklaces
- clothing—including gloves, scarves, and shoes
- musical instruments
- chariots[3]
- vases and jars
- pots made of clay[4] (they probably once contained money)
- games and toys (Tut played with them as a child)
- food and wine
- gold

Tut's tomb is a time capsule. It gives us a picture of how Egyptian kings lived more than 3000 years ago, how they died, and what they expected to need in their lives after death.

Since his discovery, Tut has not been resting in peace. He and his treasures have traveled to exhibitions around the world, where millions of visitors have been able to view some of the wonders[5] of his ancient civilization.

---

[1] **tomb:** a place where a dead body is buried; ancient Egyptian kings' tombs were very large and often had several rooms
[2] **treasure:** valuable and important objects such as gold and jewelry
[3] **chariot:** an ancient form of transportation made of wood with two wheels and pulled by a horse
[4] **clay:** heavy soil that is soft when wet, but hard when dry or baked
[5] **wonder:** an amazing thing

B. *Put the nouns from the article into the correct columns. Choose only sixteen count nouns.*

Proper Nouns	Common Nouns			
	Count Nouns		Non-Count Nouns	
1. _Tut_	1. _tomb_	9. _____	1. _furniture_	6. _____
2. _____	2. _____	10. _____	2. _____	7. _____
3. _____	3. _____	11. _____	3. _____	8. _____
4. _____	4. _____	12. _____	4. _____	9. _____
5. _____	5. _____	13. _____	5. _____	10. _____
6. _____	6. _____	14. _____		
7. _____	7. _____	15. _____		
	8. _____	16. _____		

EXERCISE 2: Noun and Verb Agreement

Complete the fact sheet with the correct form of the words in parentheses.

Did You Know . . . ?

The Pyramids

▲ Egypt's official _____ _name is_ _____ the Arab Republic
      1. (name / be)

   of Egypt.

▲ The _____ in northeastern Africa and
      2. (country / lie)

   southwestern Asia.

▲ About 17,000,000 _____ in Cairo, the capital of Egypt. It's the 11th largest
      3. (people / live)

   city in the world.

▲ _____ many interesting sites for tourists to visit, including many pyramids.
      4. (Cairo / have)

▲ _____ one of the most important export crops. _____ in
      5. (cotton / be)   **6. (rice / grow)**

   many parts of the country and is an important food crop.

▲ Most _____ Egypt during the months of October through May.
      7. (tourist / visit)

▲ The Islamic holy month of _____ from September 1 to September
      8. (Ramadan / take place)

   30. During this time many _____.
      9. (shop and restaurant / close)

▲ The _____ usually very hot in the summer. Cool, comfortable
      10. (weather / be)

   _____ important, and _____ a must.
      11. (clothing / be)   **12. (sunhat / be)**

EXERCISE 3: Quantifiers

Circle the correct words to complete this FAQ about traveling to Egypt.

Q: How many / (much) time should I spend in Cairo?
1.

A: There are so many / much things to do and see in this great city that you could easily
2.

spend a great deal of / several weeks there. Most people can't, though, so we recommend at
3.

least a little / a few days.
4.

Q: Do many / much people speak English?
5.

A: Yes. Arabic is the official language, but few / a lot of people speak English.
6.

Q: How many / much money should I take?
7.

A: In the big cities, many / few places accept credit cards, so you don't need to carry
8.

a little / much cash. There are also ATMs. But in smaller places, it's a good idea to have
9.

some / several cash or traveler's checks.
10.

Q: I'm thinking about renting a car. Is it easy to get around?

A: It's not a great idea to drive, especially in the cities. There is a lot of / several traffic. In the
11.

city, use a taxi. Cairo has a subway too.

Q: I'd like to go on a Nile River cruise. Can I book that once I'm in Egypt?

A: Yes. There are a few / few travel agencies in Cairo and Luxor that arrange tours that
12.

include boat trips.

Q: I'll need to buy any / some souvenirs to bring home. What do you recommend?
13.

A: You have little / a lot of great choices. It's always nice to bring back some / a few gold or
14.   15.

silver jewelry. You'll also find some / several beautiful cotton fabric. And don't forget to pick
16.

up some / any spices at one of the enough / many markets you'll see.
17.   18.

Q: This may seem like a strange question, but how did King Tut die?

A: Many / Much people ask that! For many / much years, historians believed Tut was killed.
19.   20.

Today there is several / a lot of evidence that he died as a result of a disease and severe
21.

injuries to his leg.

Read the posts to a travel website. There are sixteen mistakes in the use of nouns and in verb and pronoun agreement. The first mistake is already corrected. Find and correct fifteen more.

I can't tell you how much we enjoyed our trip to ~~egypt~~ *Egypt*. We just returned few days ago. What an amazing country! There are so much things to see and do. My only complaint are that we didn't have enough time! But, we'll be back!

Hannes Koch, Germany

We saw a lot of tombs and pyramids on our recent trip, but the best were the three Giza pyramids. It is huge! And, I was surprised to learn, they are located right at the edge of the city of Cairo. Because of this, there is a lot of traffic getting there (and back). There were also a lot tourists. The day we were there it was very hot. If you go, you should know that there are a few places to get anything to drink, so I REALLY recommend that you bring any water with you. Oh, and if you want to see the inside of a pyramid, you need a special ticket, and they only sell a little tickets each day. Get there early if you want one!

Vilma Ortiz, USA

The food are great in Egypt! We went to some wonderful Restaurants. We found out about one place near our hotel that doesn't have much tourists. Mostly local people eats there and everyone was really friendly. I particularly enjoyed the "meze" (a variety of appetizers). You choose a little different plates before you order your main dish. Delicious!

Jim Cook, England

There are many beautiful beach in Alexandria. A lot of them are private or connected to hotels, but there are also public ones, so be sure to bring a bathing suit if you visit that part of Egypt. The water were warm—like being in a bathtub!

Aki Kato, Japan

EXERCISE 5: Personal Writing

Imagine that you just came back from a trip. Write an email to a friend about the trip. Use some of the phrases from the box and ideas of your own.

I really liked . . .	The people . . .
I saw . . .	The weather . . .
The buildings . . .	There were . . .
The food . . .	We bought . . .

EXAMPLE: *Hi! I just got back from Lima, Peru! It's a really interesting city. The people are very friendly and . . .*

_____

_____

_____

_____

_____

_____

_____

_____

_____

_____

_____

_____

Articles: Indefinite and Definite

EXERCISE 1: Indefinite and Definite Articles

Some people are talking in school. Circle the correct words to complete the conversations. If you don't need an article, circle Ø.

1. **A:** Can I borrow a / the pen?

   B: Sure. Take a / the one on a / the desk. I don't need it.

2. **A:** Is a / the teacher here yet?

   B: No, she hasn't come yet.

3. **A:** What do you think of Mr. Mencz?

   B: He's wonderful. He's a / the best teacher I've ever had.

4. **A:** Have you done the / Ø homework?

   B: Yes. But I don't think I got a / the last answer right.

5. **A:** Could you open a / the window, please?

   B: Which one?

   A: A / The one next to a / the door.

6. **A:** Who's that?

   B: That's a / the school principal.

   A: Oh, I've never seen her before.

7. **A:** Do you like the / Ø history?

   B: It's OK. But I prefer the / Ø science. What about you?

   A: I'm very interested in a / the history of the / Ø ancient Greece.

8. **A:** We learned about an / the ozone layer in science class yesterday.

   B: Did you know there's an / the enormous "hole" in it?

   A: Yeah. It's pretty scary.

   B: It sure is. It was a / the first time I'd heard about it.

9. A: What kind of work do you do?

 B: I'm <u>an / the</u> engineer. What about you?

 A: I'm <u>a / Ø</u> mechanic.

10. A: Are they <u>some / Ø</u> students?

 B: I don't think so. They look like <u>the / Ø</u> teachers.

11. A: Do you know where I can get <u>some / the</u> water around here?

 B: Sure. There's <u>a / the</u> water fountain right across <u>a / the</u> hall, right next to <u>the / Ø</u> rest rooms.

12. A: Do you know what <u>a / the</u> homework is for tomorrow?

 B: We have to read <u>a / the</u> fable.

 A: Which one?

 B: <u>A / The</u> one on page 23.

EXERCISE 2: Indefinite and Definite Articles

*Complete the conversation. Use **a, an,** or **the** where necessary. Leave a blank if you don't need an article.*

BING YANG: Hi, Georgina. What are you doing?

GEORGINA: I'm reading _____*a*_____ fable for my English class.
                                 1.

BING YANG: What's _____ fable? I've never heard _____ word before.
                        2.   **3.**

GEORGINA: _____ fable is _____ short story about _____ animals.
                  4.   **5.**   **6.**

BING YANG: About _____ animals? Like _____ science story?
                       7.   **8.**

GEORGINA: No. It's _____ fiction. _____ animals act like _____ people. They usually
                        9.   **10.**   **11.**

 teach _____ lesson. _____ lesson is called _____ moral of _____
         12.   **13.**   **14.**   **15.**

 story, and it always comes at _____ end.
                                 16.

BING YANG: That's interesting. Who's _____ author of _____ fable you're reading?
                                          17.   **18.**

GEORGINA: Aesop. He was _____ ancient Greek writer.
                             19.

BING YANG: Oh, now I know what you're talking about. He's very famous. My parents used to

 read _____ fables to me when I was _____ child.
        20.   **21.**

GEORGINA: Well, they're also good for _____ adults. I'll lend you _____ book when I'm
                                           22.   **23.**

 finished if you're interested.

BING YANG: Thanks. I am.

*Complete this version of a famous Aesop fable. Use **a**, **an**, or **the** where necessary. Leave a blank if you don't need an article.*

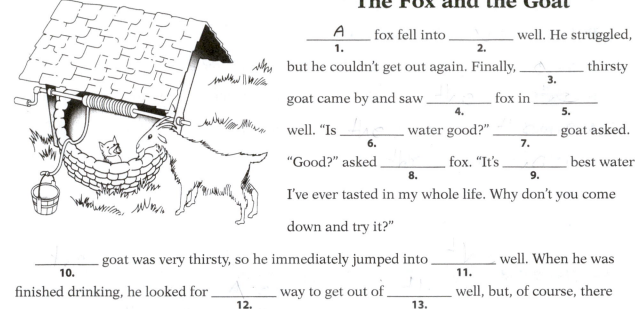

The Fox and the Goat

_____ **A** _____ fox fell into _____ well. He struggled,
1.   **2.**

but he couldn't get out again. Finally, _____ thirsty
3.

goat came by and saw _____ fox in _____
4.   **5.**

well. "Is _____ water good?" _____ goat asked.
6.   **7.**

"Good?" asked _____ fox. "It's _____ best water
8.   **9.**

I've ever tasted in my whole life. Why don't you come

down and try it?"

_____ goat was very thirsty, so he immediately jumped into _____ well. When he was
10.   **11.**

finished drinking, he looked for _____ way to get out of _____ well, but, of course, there
12.   **13.**

wasn't any. Then _____ fox said, "I have _____ excellent idea. Stand on your back legs and
14.   **15.**

place your front legs firmly against _____ front side of _____ well. Then, I'll climb onto your
16.   **17.**

back and, from there, I'll step on your horns and I'll be able to get out. When I'm out, I'll help you get

out too." _____ goat thought this was _____ good idea and followed _____ advice.
18.   **19.**   **20.**

When _____ fox was out of _____ well, he quickly and quietly walked away. _____
21.   **22.**   **23.**

goat called loudly after him and reminded him of _____ promise he had made to help him
24.

out. But _____ fox turned and said, "You should have as much sense in your head as you have
25.

_____ hairs in your beard. You jumped into _____ well before making sure you could get
26.   **27.**

out again."

MORAL: *Look before you leap.*

Complete the student's essay. There are twelve mistakes in the use of articles. The first mistake is already corrected. Find and correct eleven more.

THE FOX

A fox is ~~the~~ *a* member of the dog family. It looks like the small, thin dog with an bushy tail, a long nose, and pointed ears. You can find the foxes in most parts of a world. Animal moves very fast, and it is the very good hunter. It eats mostly mice, but it also eats the birds, insects, rabbits, and fruit.

Unfortunately, a people hunt foxes for their beautiful fur. They also hunt them for another reason. The fox is a intelligent, clever animal, and this makes it hard to catch. As a result, the hunters find it exciting to try to catch one. It is also because of its cleverness that a fox often appears in fables, such as a fable we just read in class.

EXERCISE 5: Personal Writing

Write one or two paragraphs about the fable in Exercise 3 on page 108. Did you like it? Why or why not? What is the meaning of the moral? Give an example of the importance of the moral in your own life. Use some of the phrases from the box.

I once had an experience . . .	The experience taught me . . .
I think it means . . .	The fable is about . . .
I think the fable is very . . .	The moral of the fable is . . .

EXAMPLE: *I just read the fable called "The Fox and the Goat." The fable is about a fox that . . .*

_____

_____

_____

_____

_____

_____

_____

_____

_____

_____

_____

UNIT 19 Adjectives and Adverbs

EXERCISE 1: Spelling

Write the adjectives and adverbs.

Adjectives	Adverbs
1. quick	_quickly_
2. _____.	nicely
3. fast	_____
4. good	_____
5. _____	dangerously
6. beautiful	_____
7. _____	hard
8. safe	_____
9. _____	ideally
10. _____	happily
11. _____	suddenly
12. peaceful	_____
13. angry	_____
14. _____	conveniently
15. bad	_____
16. _____	thoughtfully
17. _____	hungrily
18. extreme	_____

EXERCISE 2: Word Order: Adjectives and Adverbs

Emily is telling her friend about her new apartment. Unscramble the words to complete the conversation.

ANNA: Congratulations! _I heard about your new apartment_____.
1. (heard about / I / apartment / new / your)

EMILY: Thank you! _____!
2. (news / good / fast / travels)

ANNA: What's it like?

EMILY: _____,
3. (five / rooms / has / it / large)

_____,
4. (building / it's / large / a / very / in)

and _____.
5. (sunny / it's / very)

_____
6 . (really / we're / with it / satisfied)

ANNA: Well, it sounds ideal. How's the rent?

EMILY: _____.
7. (too / it's / bad / not)

ANNA: And what about the neighborhood?

EMILY: _____.
8. (seems / quiet / it / pretty)

The landlord is a bit of a problem, though. He's friendly and very charming, but

_____
9. (he / very / speaks / loudly)

ANNA: How come?

EMILY: _____.
10. (well / doesn't / he / hear)

ANNA: I guess nothing's perfect. I know you were looking for a long time.

_____?
11. (it / decision / was / hard / a)

EMILY: No. Not really. We really liked the apartment a lot, and it's located near school.

Besides, _____.
12. (quickly / had to / we / decide)

There were a lot of other people interested in it.

ANNA: Oh, no! Look at the time! _____.
13. (I / leave / now / have to)

_____!
14. (luck / with / good / apartment / new / your)

EMILY: Thanks. See you soon.

Emily sent an email to a friend. Complete the email with the correct form of the words in parentheses.

Hi, Lauren,

I'm _____totally_____ exhausted! James and I finished moving into our new apartment
    1. (total)
today. It was a lot of _____ work, but everything worked out _____
             2. (hard)   **3. (real)**
_____.
 4. (good)

The apartment looks very _____. It's _____ _____. The
                 5. (nice)   **6. (extreme)**   **7. (comfortable)**
only problem is with the heat. I always feel _____. We'll have to speak to the
                                     8. (cold)
landlord about it. He seems _____ _____.
                        9. (pretty)   **10. (friendly)**

People tell me that the neighborhood is very _____. That's _____
                                  11. (safe)   **12. (real)**
_____ because, as you know, I get home pretty _____ from work. I
 13. (important)   **14. (late)**
hate it when the streets are _____ _____ like they were in our old
                      15. (complete) **16. (empty)**
neighborhood.

Shopping is very _____ too. We can get to all the stores very _____.
             17. (good)   **18. (easy)**
The bus stop is located _____ the apartment, and all of the buses run
                 19. (near)
_____. Everything is _____ and _____.
 20. (frequent)   **21. (nice)**   **22. (convenient)**

Why don't you come for a visit? It would be _____ to see you.
                                23. (wonderful)

Love,

Emily

P.S. I almost _____ forgot to tell you! James got a _____ job as a
         24. (complete)   **25. (new)**
computer programmer. He feels _____ _____ about it, and that, of
                          26. (real)   **27. (happy)**
course, makes me _____ too.
            28. (happy)

Emily and James like old movies. They are going to download a few from the Internet. Circle the correct adjective forms to complete these brief movie reviews.

At Home at the Movies

BILLY BUDD Based on Herman Melville's powerful and (**1.** fascinated / fascinating) novel, this well-acted, well-produced film will leave you (**2.** disturbed / disturbing).

THE BURNING There's nothing at all (**3.** entertained / entertaining) about this 1981 horror film that takes place in a summer camp. You'll be (**4.** disgusted / disgusting) by all the blood in this story of revenge.

CHARIOTS OF FIRE Made in England, this is an (**5.** inspired / inspiring) story about two Olympic runners. Wonderfully acted.

COMING HOME Jon Voight plays the role of a (**6.** paralyzed / paralyzing) war veteran in this (**7.** moved / moving) drama about the effects of war. Powerful.

THE COMPETITION Well-acted love story about two pianists who fall in love while competing for the top prize in a music competition. You'll be (**8.** moved / moving). Beautiful music.

FOLLOW ME QUIETLY An extraordinarily (**9.** frightened / frightening) thriller about a mentally (**10.** disturbed / disturbing) man who kills people when it rains. Not for the weak-hearted.

THE GRADUATE Director Mike Nichols won an Academy Award for this funny but (**11.** touched / touching) look at a young man trying to figure out his life after college.

THE GREEN WALL Mario Robles Godoy's photography is absolutely (**12.** astonished / astonishing) in this story of a young Peruvian family. In Spanish with English subtitles.

INVASION OF THE BODY SNATCHERS One of the most (**13.** frightened / frightening) science-fiction movies ever made. You won't be (**14.** bored / boring).

WEST SIDE STORY No matter how many times you see this classic musical, you will never be (**15.** disappointed / disappointing). The story, based on Shakespeare's *Romeo and Juliet*, is (**16.** touched / touching), and the music by Leonard Bernstein is delightful and (**17.** excited / exciting).

WILBUR AND ORVILLE: THE FIRST TO FLY This is an exceptionally (**18.** entertained / entertaining) biography of the two famous Wright brothers. Good for kids too. They'll learn a lot without ever being (**19.** bored / boring).

EXERCISE 5: Word Order: Adjectives + Noun

Complete the sentences with the correct order of the words in parentheses.

1. Last night we downloaded two _____**funny old movies**_____ starring Claudio Reggiano.
   (old / funny / movies)

2. He's a(n) _____.
   (handsome / actor / tall / Italian)

3. The movie looked great on my friend's _____.
   (new / TV / large)

4. My friend served some _____.
   (delicious / pizza / mushroom / fresh)

5. We ate it on her _____.
   (leather / comfortable / black / sofa)

6. She just moved into this _____ near the college.
   (nice / apartment / small / student)

7. It's in a _____.
   (residential / quiet / neighborhood)

8. I had a very _____.
   (evening / enjoyable / relaxing)

9. I would like to find a(n) _____ like hers.
   (small / comfortable / apartment / affordable)

EXERCISE 6: Editing

Read the ad for an apartment. There are ten mistakes in the use of adjectives and adverbs.
The first one is already corrected. Find and correct nine more.

── FOR RENT ──

        Charming

~~Charmingly~~, one-bedroom apartment in a residential peaceful neighborhood.

Convenient located near shopping, transportation, entertainment, and more.

- affordable rent

- all-new appliances

- French antique beautiful desk

- friendly neighbors

- clean and safely neighborhood

- closely to park

- quiet building

This great apartment is ideal for students, and it's immediate available.

Call 444–HOME for an appointment. You won't be disappointing! But act fastly!

This apartment amazing won't last long.

EXERCISE 7: Personal Writing

Read the apartment ad in Exercise 6. Does the apartment sound good to you? Why or why not? What features are important to you in a home? Write a paragraph. Use some of the adjectives and adverbs from the box.

beautiful	good	nice	residential
convenient	inexpensive	old	safe
extremely	large	quiet	terribly
friendly	modern	really	very

EXAMPLE: *The apartment in the ad sounds very good. I like the fact that it is located in a residential neighborhood. It's really important to me to live in a quiet building . . .*

_____

_____

_____

_____

_____

_____

_____

_____

_____

_____

_____

EXERCISE 1: Spelling: Regular and Irregular Comparatives

Write the comparative forms of the adjectives.

Adjective	Comparative
1. amazing	*more amazing*
2. bad	
3. big	
4. careful	
5. cheap	
6. comfortable	
7. crowded	
8. delicious	
9. early	
10. expensive	
11. far	
12. fresh	
13. good	
14. hot	
15. noisy	
16. relaxed	
17. terrible	
18. traditional	
19. varied	
20. wet	

EXERCISE 2: Comparisons with *As . . . as*

Look at the information comparing two pizza restaurants. Complete the sentences with
just as . . . as or **not as . . . as** and the correct form of the words in parentheses.

	PIZZA PALACE	JOE'S PIZZERIA
Year opened	2000	2000
Number of tables	40	20
Pizza size	12 inches	12 inches
Price of a cheese pizza	$8.00	$8.00
Choice of pizza toppings	15	7
Average waiting time for a table	10 minutes	5 minutes
Hours	noon–11:00 P.M. (7 days a week)	noon–8:00 P.M. (closed Mondays)
Atmosphere	★★	★
Service	★★	★★
Cleanliness	★★	★★
Food	★★	★★★

1. The Pizza Palace is _____*just as old as*_____ Joe's Pizzeria.
   (old)

2. Joe's Pizzeria is _____ the Pizza Palace.
   (large)

3. A pizza from Joe's Pizzeria is _____ one from the Pizza Palace.
   (big)

4. The pizza at the Pizza Palace is _____ the pizza at Joe's Pizzeria.
   (expensive)

5. The choice of toppings at Joe's Pizzeria is _____ the choice at the
   (varied)

   Pizza Palace.

6. The waiting time at Joe's Pizzeria is _____ it is at the Pizza Palace.
   (long)

7. The hours at Joe's Pizzeria are _____ the hours at the Pizza Palace.
   (convenient)

8. Closing hour at Joe's Pizzeria is _____ it is at the Pizza Palace.
   (late)

9. The atmosphere at Joe's Pizzeria is _____ it is at the Pizza Palace.
   (nice)

10. The service at Joe's Pizzeria is _____ the service at the Pizza Palace.
    (good)

11. The pizza at the Pizza Palace is _____ it is at Joe's Pizzeria.
    (good)

12. Joe's Pizzeria is _____ the Pizza Palace.
    (clean)

These conversations took place at the Pizza Palace. Complete the conversations with the correct form of the adjectives in parentheses. Use **than** when necessary.

1. **A:** Wow, this place has gotten really popular!

   B: I know. It's even _____<u>more popular than</u>_____ Joe's Pizzeria.
   (popular)

2. **A:** I can't believe how long the line is!

   B: Maybe we should come for an _____ dinner next time.
   (early)

3. **A:** I prefer that table over there.

   B: Me too. It looks _____.
   (comfortable)

4. **A:** Let's order pizza number 7—with spinach, mushrooms, and tomatoes.

   B: OK. That sounds _____ the one with pepperoni and extra cheese.
   (healthy)

5. **A:** Mmm. This pizza is delicious. It's _____ the traditional kind.
   (interesting)

   B: It *is* good, but I still think the pizza at Joe's is even _____ the
   (good)

   pizza here. And Joe's ingredients always seem somewhat _____
   (fresh)

   to me. Anyhow, that's just my opinion.

6. **A:** Hey, is that Brian over there at that table?

   B: No. Brian is much _____ that guy.
   (tall)

7. **A:** It sure is noisy in here. It's probably _____ on weekends.
   (bad)

   B: But it's a lot _____ at Joe's! And the atmosphere is
   (quiet)

   _____ too.
   (relaxed)

8. **A:** It's already 8:00.

   B: Oh! I thought it was _____ that.
   (late)

9. **A:** Do you ever make pizza yourself?

   B: No. I buy it frozen. It's _____ just to pop it in the microwave.
   (fast)

10. **A:** I really should buy a microwave oven.

    B: You really should. It will make your life _____.
    (easy)

Look at the chart comparing two microwave ovens. Complete the sentences with the appropriate comparative form of the adjectives in parentheses and **than.** *Also, fill in the blanks with the brand—***X** *or* **Y.**

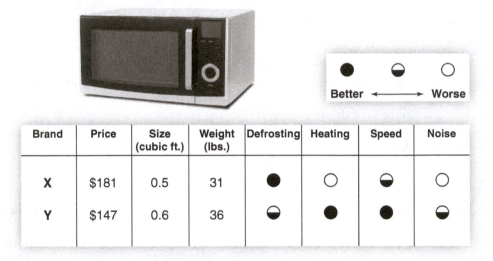

Better ←——→ Worse

Brand	Price	Size (cubic ft.)	Weight (lbs.)	Defrosting	Heating	Speed	Noise
X	$181	0.5	31	●	○	◗	○
Y	$147	0.6	36	◗	●	●	◗

1. Brand ___X___ is ___more expensive than___ Brand ___Y___.
            (expensive)

2. Brand _____ is _____ Brand _____.
            (cheap)

3. Brand _____ is _____ Brand _____.
            (large)

4. Brand _____ is _____ Brand _____.
            (small)

5. Brand _____ is _____ Brand _____.
            (heavy)

6. Brand _____ is _____ Brand _____.
            (light)

7. For defrosting food, Brand _____ is _____ Brand _____.
            (efficient)

8. For heating food, Brand _____ is _____ Brand _____.
            (effective)

9. Brand _____ is _____ Brand _____.
            (fast)

10. Brand _____ is _____ Brand _____.
             (slow)

11. Brand _____ is _____ Brand _____.
             (noisy)

12. Brand _____ is _____ Brand _____.
             (quiet)

13. In general, Brand _____ seems _____ Brand _____.
             (good)

14. In general, Brand _____ seems _____ Brand _____.
             (bad)

EXERCISE 5: Comparatives to Express Increase or Decrease

*Look at the chart. It shows some food trends (increases and decreases). Complete the statements about the trends. Use the comparative forms of the adjectives from the box to show an increase or a decrease, or a cause and effect. Use both **more** and **less**.*

| big | cheap | ~~expensive~~ | good | healthy | heavy | popular | varied |

	1995	2005	2010
1. cost of a slice of pizza	$	$$	$$$
2. cost of a microwave oven	$$$	$$	$
3. quality of frozen pizza	+	++	+++
4. restaurant portion size	+	++	+++
5. choice of pizza toppings	+	++	+++
6. popularity of fast food	+	++	+++
7. health quality of fast food	+++	++	+
8. weight of fast-food customers	+	++	+++

1. A slice of pizza is getting _____ *more and more expensive* _____.

2. A microwave oven is getting _____.

3. The quality of frozen pizza is getting _____.

4. The size of portions in restaurants is getting _____.

5. The choice of pizza toppings is getting _____.

6. Fast food is becoming _____.

7. It's also becoming _____.

8. Fast-food customers are becoming _____.

EXERCISE 6: Cause and Effect with Two Comparatives

Read the information. Write a similar sentence using two comparatives.

1. When the pizza is salty, I get thirsty.

   The saltier the pizza, the thirstier I get.

2. When the ingredients are fresh, the food is good.

   _____

(continued on next page)

3. When the restaurant is popular, the lines are long.

_____

4. When the meal is enjoyable, the customers are satisfied.

_____

5. When the selection is big, the customers are happy.

_____

6. When it's late in the day, the servers get tired.

_____

7. When the restaurant is crowded, the service is slow.

_____

8. When the service is good, the tip is high.

_____

EXERCISE 7: Editing

Read the journal entry. There are eight mistakes in the use of comparisons. The first one is already corrected. Find and correct seven more.

I just got home from the Pizza Palace. Wow! The pizza there just keeps getting ~~good~~ **better**

and better. And, of course, the better the food, the more long the lines, and the

crowdeder the restaurant! But I don't really mind. It's totally worth it. Tonight Ana and

I shared a pizza with spinach, mushrooms, and fresher tomatoes. It was much more

interesting as a traditional pizza with just tomato sauce and cheese. It's also healthier

than. And the ingredients were as fresh than you can find anywhere in the city.

(Although I usually think the pizza at Joe's Pizzeria is fresher.) It was so large that

we couldn't finish it, so I brought the rest home. Actually, I'm getting hungry again just

thinking about it. I think I'll pop a slice into the microwave and warm it up. It will

probably taste almost as better as it tasted at the Pizza Palace!

EXERCISE 8: Personal Writing

What is your opinion? Write a paragraph about two meals you have recently eaten. Compare the experiences. Where did you eat? What did you have? How did you like it? Use the comparative form of some of the adjectives from the box.

big	fast	healthy	noisy
expensive	good	interesting	relaxing

EXAMPLE: *Recently, I ate in the school cafeteria. It was better than I expected. I had a chicken sandwich and a cup of tomato soup. The food was a lot cheaper than the food at the corner restaurant, and many of the choices were much . . .*

_____

_____

_____

_____

_____

_____

_____

_____

_____

_____

_____

_____

Adjectives: Superlatives

EXERCISE 1: Spelling: Regular and Irregular Superlatives

Write the superlative form of the adjectives.

Adjective	Superlative
1. amazing	*the most amazing*
2. bad	
3. big	
4. cute	
5. dynamic	
6. expensive	
7. far	
8. funny	
9. good	
10. happy	
11. hot	
12. important	
13. intelligent	
14. interesting	
15. low	
16. nice	
17. noisy	
18. practical	
19. warm	
20. wonderful	

EXERCISE 2: The Superlative

Look at the information comparing the subway systems in three cities. Complete the sentences with the superlative form of the adjectives in parentheses. Also, write the name of the correct city.

THREE NORTH AMERICAN SUBWAY SYSTEMS			
	Toronto	**New York City**	**Mexico City**
First opened	1954	1904	1969
Length (miles)	42.4	229	109.6
Number of riders (per year)	280 million	1.6 billion	1.4 billion
Cost of a single ride*	$2.94	$2.25	$0.24

*in U.S. dollars

1. ___New York City___ has ___the oldest___ subway system.
   (old)

2. _____ has _____ subway system.
   (new)

3. _____'s system is _____.
   (long)

4. _____'s system is _____.
   (short)

5. _____ system is in _____.
   (busy)

6. _____ has _____ number of riders.
   (low)

7. The subway in _____ is _____ to use.
   (expensive)

8. You can buy _____ single ticket in _____.
   (cheap)

EXERCISE 3: Superlative Adjectives

Read the comments posted on an online subway message board. Complete the sentences with the superlative form of the correct adjectives from the boxes. Use **the -est** *or* **the most / the least**.

Track Talk

| beautiful | big | easy | new | ~~old~~ |

I just got back from London. Completed in 1863, the Tube (that's what they call their

subway) is _____ *the oldest* _____ in the world, but it works just fine!
    1.

Completed just a few years ago, Sheppard Subway is _____
               2.

metro line in Toronto. I just rode it. Very nice!

IMHO (In my humble[1] opinion), the Moscow subway stations are without question

_____ in the world. They have some really nice features.
   3.

Statues, chandeliers, and artwork on the walls make them look more like museums than

stations! It's also one of _____ systems to use. There are plenty
       4.

of maps and signs in the stations so you don't get lost. As you can see, I'm one of

_____ fans of this great public transportation system!
   5.

| comfortable | convenient | cool | dangerous | fast | hot | interesting |

I just got back from a week's vacation in New York City. We had a great time and rode

the subway a lot. I have to say the subway seats are _____ I've
          6.

ever experienced! They are so hard. I heard they used to be made of straw.[2] In any case,

it's _____ way to get around town—no traffic to slow you
   7.

down. It's summer, and all the trains are air-conditioned. Get ready for one of

---

[1] *humble:* not considering your ideas as important or as good as other people's
[2] *straw:* dried stems of wheat or similar plants

_____ rides you've ever been on. In contrast, the stations are
8.

among _____ I've ever been in. I'm sure the temperature was
9.

over 100 degrees. That said, New York has one of _____
10.

systems in the world. It's open 24 hours a day, 7 days a week, and you can go all over the

place—even to the beach! And I think it's _____ form of
11.

transportation to take. You see all kinds of people. It's a very multicultural experience.

Really fascinating. And this may really surprise you, but some people say it's one of

_____ subway systems because there are so many people on it.
12.

You're almost never alone—even late at night. I guess there's safety in numbers!

| crowded | dangerous | efficient | expensive | historic | quiet |

The subway in Athens is probably _____ in the world. When
13.

they were building the system, they found the remains of ancient roads, shops, and baths.

They've made these part of the system.

Tokyo has _____ subway in the world. At rush hour, there are
14.

so many people, special workers help push them onto the trains!

Driving in Paris? Don't even think about it! _____ way of
15.

getting around is the Metro. As in all big cities, you need to be careful and watch your

stuff. Rush hour is definitely _____ time to ride the subway
16.

because there can be pickpockets "working" the trains.

I love the subway system in Mexico City. First of all, at just 3 pesos (about 25 cents), it's

_____ ride in town (actually, in the whole world!). And because
17.

the train has rubber wheels, it's one of _____ rides too.
18.

EXERCISE 4: Editing

Read the tourist's postcard. There are seven mistakes in the use of the superlative. The first mistake is already corrected. Find and correct six more.

Hola!

Greetings from Mexico City! With its mixture of the old and the new, this is one of the ~~interestingest~~ *most interesting* cities I've ever visited. The people are among the friendlier in the world, and they have

been very patient with my attempts to speak their language. Spanish is definitely one of a most beautiful languages, and I really want to take lessons when I get home. This has been the most hot summer in years, and I'm looking forward to going to the beach next week. The air pollution is also the baddest I've experienced, so I'll be glad to be out of the city. By the way, we definitely did not need to rent a car. The most fast and convenientest way to get around is by subway.

See you soon.

L.

EXERCISE 5: Personal Writing

Write a paragraph about your city or country. What are some of the best things about it? The worst? Use the superlative form of some of the adjectives from the box.

affordable	clean	easy	interesting
bad	convenient	friendly	nice
beautiful	difficult	good	safe

EXAMPLE: *One of the best things about living here is the people. They are among the friendliest and most interesting people I've ever met . . .*

_____

_____

_____

_____

_____

_____

_____

_____

_____

_____

_____

UNIT 22 Adverbs: *As . . . as*, Comparatives, Superlatives

EXERCISE 1: Spelling: Regular and Irregular Comparative and Superlative Forms of Adverbs

Write the comparative and superlative forms of the adverbs.

Adverb	Comparative	Superlative
1. aggressively	more aggressively	the most aggressively
2. badly		
3. beautifully		
4. carefully		
5. consistently		
6. dangerously		
7. early		
8. effectively		
9. far		
10. fast		
11. frequently		
12. hard		
13. intensely		
14. little		
15. long		
16. much		
17. quickly		
18. slowly		
19. soon		
20. well		

EXERCISE 2: Comparisons of Adverbs with *As . . . as*

Look at the track-and-field records for five athletes. Complete the statements with the words in parentheses and (**not**) **as . . . as.**

	100-METER RUN	HIGH JUMP	DISCUS THROW
Athlete A	12.0 sec.	1.8 m	37 m
Athlete B	14.0 sec.	1.6 m	39 m
Athlete C	13.5 sec.	1.9 m	38 m
Athlete D	14.0 sec.	1.9 m	39 m
Athlete E	15.0 sec.	2.0 m	40 m

1. Athlete B ____*didn't run as fast as*____ Athlete A.
   (run / fast)

2. Athlete B _____ Athlete D.
   (run / fast)

3. Athlete C _____ Athlete D.
   (jump / high)

4. Athlete A _____ Athlete E.
   (jump / high)

5. Athlete C _____ Athlete E.
   (throw the discus / far)

6. Athlete D _____ Athlete B.
   (throw the discus / far)

7. In general, Athlete B _____ Athlete D.
   (do / good)

8. In general, Athlete A _____ Athlete C.
   (compete / successful)

EXERCISE 3: The Comparative Form of Adverbs

Basketball players from two teams are talking about their last game. Complete their comments. Use the correct form of the words in parentheses. Use **than** *when necessary.*

GEORGE: The other team played well, but we played much ____*better*____. That's
        1. (good)

why we won.

JAMIL: We played _____ our opponents. We really deserved to win,
        2. (hard)

and we did.

(continued on next page)

ALEX: It wasn't a great game for me. I moved _____ usual because of

3. (slow)

my bad ankle. In a few weeks, I should be able to run _____. I

4. (fast)

hope that'll help the team.

RICK: Our shooting was off today. We missed too many baskets. We need to shoot a lot

_____ if we want to win.

5. (consistent)

⊕ ⊕ ⊕ ⊕

LARRY: I was surprised by how well they played. They played _____

6. (aggressive)

they've played in a long time. We couldn't beat them.

⊕ ⊕ ⊕ ⊕

ELVIN: I'm disappointed. We've really been playing a lot _____ our

7. (bad)

opponents this season. We have to try to concentrate _____ in

8. (good)

order to break this losing streak.

⊕ ⊕ ⊕ ⊕

RANDY: Team spirit was very strong. We played a lot _____ together,

9. (effective)

and it paid off.

⊕ ⊕ ⊕ ⊕

CARLOS: Of course I'm happy with the results. But if we want to keep it up, we have to practice

_____ and _____. I think we just got

10. (intense)   11. (frequent)

lucky today.

Now write the names of the players under the correct team.

Winning Team	**Losing Team**
George	_____
_____	_____
_____	_____
_____	_____

EXERCISE 4: The Comparative and the Superlative of Adverbs

*Look at the chart in Exercise 2 on page 131. Complete the statements with the correct form of the words in parentheses. Use **than** when necessary. Then complete the statements with the letter of the correct athlete—**A, B, C, D,** or **E.***

1. Athlete B ran _____*faster than*_____ Athlete __E__, but Athlete __A__ ran
   (fast)
   _____*the fastest*_____ of all.
   (fast)

2. Athlete _____ ran _____. He ran _____ all
   (slow)   (slow)
   the other competitors.

3. Athlete A jumped _____ Athlete _____.
   (high)

4. Athlete _____ jumped _____ of all five athletes.
   (high)

5. Athletes B and D didn't throw the discus _____ Athlete _____.
   (far)

6. Athlete _____ threw the discus _____.
   (far)

7. Athlete _____ won in two categories. He performed _____.
   (good)

8. At 15 seconds, Athlete _____ scored _____ in the run, but he did
   (bad)
   _____ the other athletes in the rest of the events.
   (good)

EXERCISE 5: The Comparative of Adverbs to Express Change

Read about some athletes. Write a summary statement about each situation. Use the correct form of the words from the box.

accurate	dangerous	~~fast~~	graceful	long
bad	~~far~~	frequent	high	slow

1. Last month Lisa ran a mile in 12 minutes. This month she's running a mile in 8 minutes.

   SUMMARY: _*She's running faster and faster.*_____

2. Last month she ran three times a week. This month she's running every day.

   SUMMARY: _____

3. Last month Josh threw the ball 10 yards. This month he's throwing it 13 yards.

   SUMMARY: _____

(continued on next page)

4. Last month when Jennifer shot baskets, she got only five balls in. Now when she shoots baskets, she gets at least eight balls in.

SUMMARY: _____

5. Six months ago, Mike jumped 4½ feet. Now he's jumping almost 6 feet.

SUMMARY: _____

6. Matt used to run an 8-minute mile. These days he runs a 10-minute mile.

SUMMARY: _____

7. The ice-dancing team of Sonia and Boris used to score about 30 points for their program. These days they are scoring more than 40 points.

SUMMARY: _____

8. The basketball team used to practice two hours a day. Now they practice three.

SUMMARY: _____

9. Jason drives a race car. Last year he had two accidents. This year he's had five.

SUMMARY: _____

10. Last year the team felt good about their game. Now they feel terrible.

SUMMARY: _____

EXERCISE 6: Editing

Read Luisa's online exercise journal. There are seven mistakes in the use of adverbs. The first mistake is already corrected. Find and correct six more.

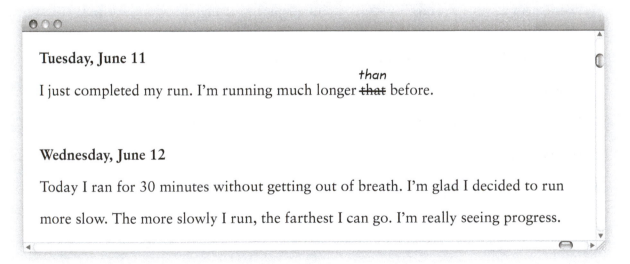

Tuesday, June 11

I just completed my run. I'm running much longer ~~that~~ *than* before.

Wednesday, June 12

Today I ran for 30 minutes without getting out of breath. I'm glad I decided to run more slow. The more slowly I run, the farthest I can go. I'm really seeing progress.

Thursday, June 13

Because I'm enjoying it, I run more and more frequent. And the more often I do it, the longer and farther I can go. I really believe that running helps me feel better more quick than other forms of exercise. I'm even sleeping better than before!

Friday, June 14

I'm thinking about running in the next marathon. I may not run as fast than younger runners, but I think I can run long and farther. We'll see!

EXERCISE 7: Personal Writing

Write a paragraph about your English skills. How are you speaking? Are you understanding what you hear? How is your reading? Writing? Use the adverb forms of the words from the box (or your own ideas).

accurate	fluent	hard
easy	frequent	quick
fast	good	slow

EXAMPLE: *I think my English skills are really improving. I'm speaking more fluently, and . . .*

_____

_____

_____

_____

_____

_____

_____

_____

_____

_____

_____

_____

PART VII

GERUNDS AND INFINITIVES

UNIT 23 Gerunds: Subject and Object

EXERCISE 1: Gerunds as Subject and as Object

Complete the article from a health magazine. Use the gerund form of the verbs in parentheses.

KICK UP YOUR HEELS!

In recent years, _____dancing_____ has become a very popular
1. (dance)

way to stay in shape. In addition to its health benefits, it also has

social advantages. "I really enjoy _____ out and
2. (go)

_____ new people," says Diana Romero, a twenty-eight-year-old word
3. (meet)

processor. "_____ all day at a computer isn't healthy. After work I need to
4. (sit)

move." And Diana isn't alone on the dance floor. Many people who dislike

_____, _____ weights, or _____ sit-ups are
5. (run)   **6. (lift)**   **7. (do)**

swaying to the beat of the swing, salsa, and rumba.

   So, if you are looking for an enjoyable way to build muscles and friendships, consider

_____ a spin on one of the many studio dance floors that are opening up in
8. (take)

cities across the country. "_____ can be fun," says Sandra Carrone, owner
9. (exercise)

of Studio Two-Step. So, quit _____ time, grab a partner, and kick up your
10. (waste)

heels!

EXERCISE 2: Gerunds as Subject and as Object

Look at the results of this questionnaire on four students' likes and dislikes. Then complete the sentences below with appropriate gerunds.

Key: + enjoy
     ✓ don't mind
     − dislike

	KATIE	RYAN	LUKE	ANA
Dance	+	+	+	+
Walk	+	+	✓	✓
Do sit-ups	−	−	−	−
Play tennis	+	−	+	✓
Run	−	+	+	+
Lift weights	−	✓	−	+
Swim	✓	+	−	✓
Ride a bike	+	+	✓	+

1. Ryan is the only one who dislikes _____ *playing tennis* _____.

2. _____ is the group's favorite activity.

3. Half the people dislike _____.

4. Half the people enjoy _____ and _____.

5. Katie and Ana don't mind _____.

6. Ana is the only one who enjoys _____.

7. Luke doesn't mind _____ or _____.

8. _____ is the most disliked activity.

9. Luke is the only one who dislikes _____.

10. He also doesn't like _____ or _____.

11. Katie is the only one who doesn't like _____.

12. Katie and Luke really like _____, but Ryan dislikes it.

13. _____ is the group's second favorite activity.

14. Ryan doesn't mind _____.

EXERCISE 3: Gerunds after Certain Verbs

Sandra Carrone is having a dance party at her studio. Complete the summary sentences with the appropriate verbs from the box and the gerund form of the verbs in parentheses.

admit	consider	dislike	keep	permit	regret
ban	deny	enjoy	mind	~~quit~~	suggest

1. **LUKE:** Would you like a cup of coffee?

   KATIE: No, thanks. I haven't had coffee in five years.

   SUMMARY: Katie _____*quit drinking*_____ coffee five years ago.

   (drink)

2. **OSCAR:** Oh, they're playing a tango. Would you like to dance?

   RIKA: No, thanks. It's not my favorite dance.

   SUMMARY: Rika _____ the tango.

   (do)

3. **ANA:** Do you often come to these dance parties?

   MARIA: Yes. It's a good opportunity to dance with a lot of different partners.

   SUMMARY: Maria _____ with different partners.

   (dance)

4. **LAURA:** I don't know how to do the cha-cha. Could you show me?

   BILL: OK. Just follow me.

   SUMMARY: Bill doesn't _____ Laura the cha-cha.

   (teach)

5. **KATIE:** This is a difficult dance. How did you learn it?

   LUKE: I practiced it over and over again.

   SUMMARY: Luke _____ the dance.

   (practice)

6. **VERA:** Ow. You stepped on my toe!

   LUIS: No, I didn't!

   SUMMARY: Luis _____ on Vera's toe.

   (step)

7. **BILL:** Are you going to take any more classes?

   LAURA: I'm not sure. I haven't decided yet. Maybe.

   SUMMARY: Laura is _____ more dance classes.

   (take)

8. **KATIE:** I really love dancing.

   LUKE: Me too. I'm sorry I didn't start years ago. It's a lot of fun.

   SUMMARY: Luke _____ dance lessons sooner.
   (not begin)

9. **BILL:** Why don't we go out for coffee after class next week?

   LAURA: OK. I'd like that.

   SUMMARY: Bill _____ out after class.
   (go)

10. **LUKE:** You look tired.

    LAURA: I *am* tired. I think this will be the last dance for me.

    SUMMARY: Laura _____ tired.
    (feel)

11. **DAN:** Would you like a cigarette?

    INA: I don't smoke. Besides, it isn't permitted here.

    SUMMARY: The studio _____.
    (smoke)

12. **DAN:** You can't smoke in the studio?

    INA: No. But you can smoke outside.

    SUMMARY: The studio _____ outside.
    (smoke)

EXERCISE 4: Gerunds after Prepositions

Complete the conversations with the correct preposition and the gerund form of the verbs in parentheses.

1. **KYLE:** Where were you? It's 7:30!

   JOHN: I know. I apologize _____ *for being* _____ late.
   (be)

2. **EMMA:** Are you excited about your vacation?

   JUSTIN: Oh, yes. I'm really looking forward _____ a
   (have)
   break. I need one.

3. **AUSTIN:** I'm trying to stop smoking, but it's so hard.

   NOAH: Don't give up. I'm sure you'll succeed _____.
   (quit)

4. **RYAN:** What's wrong? You look upset.

   SASHA: I have a test tomorrow, and I'm worried _____ it.
   (pass)

(continued on next page)

5. **CHENG:** Where's José?

   COLE: He's still at work. He insisted _____ late and

   _____ (stay)

   _____ his report.
   (finish)

6. **KEVIN:** I'm tired _____ home every night. Let's go out.
   (stay)

   AMBER: Good idea. I'm in favor _____ out more.
   (get)

7. **KAYLA:** I hear the school cafeteria is going to get a salad bar.

   MEGAN: That' s great. I believe _____ healthy choices for
   (have)

   lunch. It's important.

8. **JOHN:** Do you approve _____ smoking outside the
   (permit)

   school building?

   SIMON: Actually, I don't. I'm opposed _____ in public
   (smoke)

   areas. They should prohibit it.

EXERCISE 5: Editing

Read the online survey about smoking. There are seven mistakes in the use of gerunds. The first one is already corrected. Find and correct six more.

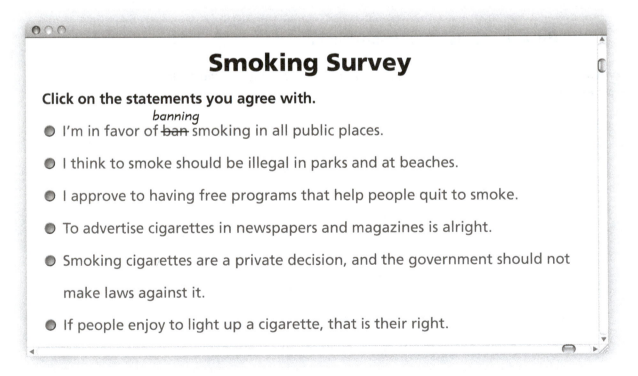

Smoking Survey

Click on the statements you agree with.

       banning
○ I'm in favor of ~~ban~~ smoking in all public places.

○ I think to smoke should be illegal in parks and at beaches.

○ I approve to having free programs that help people quit to smoke.

○ To advertise cigarettes in newspapers and magazines is alright.

○ Smoking cigarettes are a private decision, and the government should not

   make laws against it.

○ If people enjoy to light up a cigarette, that is their right.

EXERCISE 6: Personal Writing

Look at the chart in Exercise 2 on page 137. How do you feel about the eight activities in the chart? Write a paragraph. Use some of the phrases from the box.

I can get tired of . . .	I really dislike . . .
I can't get excited about . . .	I sometimes look forward to . . .
I don't enjoy . . .	I would like to start . . .
I don't mind . . .	I'm not opposed to . . .
I enjoy . . .	I've never considered . . .

EXAMPLE: *I know exercise is important. I try to do some every day, but there are some things I like better than others. Dancing is my favorite activity. I enjoy . . .*

_____

_____

_____

_____

_____

_____

_____

_____

_____

_____

_____

Infinitives after Certain Verbs

EXERCISE 1: Infinitives after Certain Verbs

Read the exchange of letters in an advice column. Complete the letters with the correct form of the verbs in parentheses. Use the simple present, simple past, or future for the first verb.

Dear Annie,

I've known John for two years. We share a lot of similar interests, and until recently got along great. Last month, we _____**decided to get**_____ engaged. Since then, our relationship

1. (decide / get)

has been a nightmare. John criticizes me for every little thing. I

_____ a marriage counselor, but John

2. (want / see)

_____ with me. Last night, he even

3. (refuse / go)

_____ the relationship if I mention the idea of counseling again.

4. (threaten / end)

I don't understand what's going on. I still love John, but I _____

5. (hesitate / take)

the next step. Can we solve our problems? What should I do?

ONE FOOT OUT THE DOOR

Dear One Foot Out the Door,

I've heard your story many times before. You're right to be concerned. Obviously, John

_____afraid of getting married. As soon as you got engaged, he

6. (seem / be)

_____ distance by criticizing you. I agree that counseling is a good

7. (attempt / create)

idea if the two of you really _____ together. Maybe each of you

8. (intend / stay)

_____ to a counselor separately before going to one together. It's

9. (need / speak)

possible that John _____ alone to discuss some of his fears.

10. (agree / go)

ANNIE

EXERCISE 2: Verb + Infinitive or Verb + Object + Infinitive

Read the conversations between men and women in relationships. Complete the two summary statements for each conversation.

1. **SHE:** We need to focus on our relationship. I *really* think we should see a therapist.

    HE: Well, I'm not going to.

    SUMMARY: She urged *him to see a therapist.* _____

    He refused *to see a therapist.* _____

2. **HE:** Could you please do the dishes tonight?

    SHE: Sorry. I don't have time. Could *you* please do them?

    SUMMARY: He didn't want _____

    She wanted _____

3. **HE:** Don't forget to buy some milk.

    SHE: OK. I'll get some on the way home.

    SUMMARY: He reminded _____

    She agreed _____

4. **SHE:** Will you do me a favor? Could you drive me to my aunt's?

    HE: OK.

    SUMMARY: She asked _____

    He agreed _____

5. **SHE:** Would you like to have dinner at my place Friday night?

    HE: Um . . . I'm not sure. Um . . . I guess so.

    SUMMARY: She invited _____

    He hesitated _____

6. **SHE:** Will you give me your answer tomorrow?

    HE: Yes, I will. That's a promise.

    SUMMARY: She wants _____

    He promised _____

(continued on next page)

7. **SHE:** Would you like me to cut your hair? It's really long.

    HE: Oh, OK.

    SUMMARY: She offered _____

    He is going to allow _____

8. **SHE:** It's 8:00. I thought you said you'd be home at 7:00.

    HE: No. I always get home at 8:00.

    SUMMARY: She expected _____

    He expected _____

9. **HE:** Why didn't you call me before you left the office?

    SHE: I was going to, but I forgot.

    SUMMARY: He wanted _____

    She intended _____

10. **SHE:** Let's see a movie Friday night.

    HE: OK, but could you pick one out?

    SUMMARY: She would like _____

    He would like _____

11. **HE:** I plan on asking my boss for a raise.

    SHE: Great idea. I think you definitely should do it.

    SUMMARY: He intends _____

    She's encouraging _____

12. **SHE:** I'd like to get some more stamps.

    HE: Oh, I'll stop at the post office on the way home.

    SUMMARY: She wants _____

    He volunteered _____

EXERCISE 3: Editing

Read the journal entry. There are ten mistakes in the use of infinitives. The first mistake is already corrected. Find and correct nine more.

Annie answered my letter. I didn't expect ~~hearing~~ *to hear* back from her so soon! She agrees that seeing a counselor is a good idea for John and me, but she advised we to go to counseling separately at first. That idea never even occurred to me, but I think that it's a really excellent suggestion. I don't know if John will agree going, but I'm definitely going to ask him to think about it when I see him on Saturday. I attempted to introduce the topic last night, but he pretended to not hear me. (He's been doing that a lot lately. He seems to think if he ignores a question, I'll just forget about it!) I won't give up, though. I'm going to try to persuade he to go. I have no idea how to find a counselor, so if he agrees to go, I may ask Annie recommend some in our area. Obviously, I want finding someone really good.

I still believe in us as a couple. Our relationship deserves to have a chance, and I'm prepared give it one. But I want John feels the same way. After all, it takes more than one person to make a relationship. I really need to know that he's 100 percent committed to the relationship. I can be patient, but I can't afford waiting forever.

EXERCISE 4: Personal Writing

What do you expect from your friends? Write one or two paragraphs. Use some of the phrases from the box or ideas of your own.

I count on them . . .	I prefer (them) . . .
I don't expect them . . .	I really need (them) . . .
I expect my friends . . .	I would like (them) . . .

EXAMPLE: *Friends are really important to me. I expect my friends to always tell me the truth. When I have a problem, I count on them . . .*

_____

_____

_____

_____

_____

_____

_____

_____

_____

_____

_____

UNIT 25 More Uses of Infinitives

EXERCISE 1: Infinitives of Purpose: Affirmative Statements

Look at the chart. Make sentences with the words in parentheses.

SOME FUNCTIONS OF MOBILE DEVICES			
	CELL PHONE	SMART PHONE	PDA
make calls	●	●	●
take pictures	●	●	
search online		●	
send email		●	
connect to the Internet	●	●	●
create a "To Do" list		●	●
store addresses	●	●	●
play music		●	
translate words		●	

NOTE: Technology changes fast, so it is possible that today you can use these devices to do a lot more things!

1. *You can use cell phones and smart phones to make calls.*
   (make calls)

2. _____
   (take pictures)

3. _____
   (search online)

4. _____
   (send email)

5. _____
   (connect to the Internet)

6. _____
   (create a "To Do" list)

7. _____
   (store addresses)

8. _____
   (play music)

9. _____
   (translate words)

EXERCISE 2: Infinitives of Purpose: Affirmative and Negative Statements

Combine these pairs of sentences. Use the infinitive of purpose.

1. Ned got a job at Edge Electronics. He needs to earn money for school.

   Ned got a job at Edge Electronics to earn money for school.

2. Ned never brings money to work. He doesn't want to buy a lot of stuff.

   Ned never brings money to work in order not to buy a lot of stuff.

3. He uses most of his salary. He has to pay his college tuition.

   _____

4. He really wants an MP3 player. He wants to download music from the Internet.

   _____

5. He's going to wait for a sale. Then he won't pay the full price.

   _____

6. A lot of people came into the store today. They looked at the new multipurpose devices.

   _____

7. They like talking to Ned. They want to get information about the devices.

   _____

8. Someone bought a GPS. He doesn't want to get lost.

   _____

9. Another person bought a tiny camcorder. She wants to bring it on vacation.

   _____

10. She used her credit card. She didn't want to pay right away.

    _____

11. Ned showed her how to use the camcorder. It can do a lot of things.

    _____

12. She'll use it as a camera. She'll take videos.

    _____

EXERCISE 3: Infinitives after Adjectives

Some people are talking at a mall. Complete the conversations with the verbs from the box and the infinitive of purpose.

eat	find	have	~~keep up~~	leave	pay	take

1. A: I need to go to Edge Electronics.

    B: How come?

    A: I've decided to get a new smart phone. It's important _____*to keep up*_____ with

    the latest technology!

2. A: I'd like to return this PDA.

    B: Do you have the receipt?

    A: No, I don't. I got it as a gift.

    B: Hmmm. I see that there's no price tag on it. I'm very sorry, but it's necessary

    _____ the receipt in order to return it.

3. A: Why don't you use your credit card?

    B: I know it's convenient _____ with a credit card, but I prefer to use

    cash for small purchases. Call me old-fashioned!

4. A: I'm hungry. How's the food court here?

    B: It's actually very nice _____ there. The food is pretty good and

    there's a great view of the capitol building.

5. A: That was a good lunch. I'm ready _____ now. What about you?

    B: Sure. I'm done shopping. Let's go.

6. A: Well, here's the escalator.

    B: It's faster _____ the elevator. And it's right over there.

7. A: Do you want to see a movie?

    B: OK. But we don't have a schedule with us.

    A: No problem! I have my smart phone. It's easy _____ a movie

    with it. Let's see what's playing around here.

EXERCISE 4: Infinitives after Adjectives and Adverbs + *Too* or *Enough*

Complete the conversations. Use the words in parentheses with the infinitive and **too** or **enough**.

1. **A:** Did you get a new smart phone at the mall?

   B: No. It was still _____too expensive for me to get_____.
   (expensive / me / get)

2. **A:** Are you really that unhappy with the phone you have now?

   B: Not really. It's _____ most everything I need to do.
   (good / me / do)

   I just would like it to have some more functions.

3. **A:** Do you want to go to a movie tonight?

   B: It's 10:00 already. It's _____.
   (late / go)

4. **A:** Maybe we can go tomorrow night.

   B: Sure, if we finish dinner _____ by 7:00.
   (fast / leave)

5. **A:** I have an idea. Why don't we combine a movie with a late-night dinner afterward?

   B: OK. That is, if I'm not _____ awake!
   (tired / stay)

6. **A:** Do you think I can call Alicia now?

   B: At 10:00? Sure. It's not _____.
   (late / call)

7. **A:** Do you have trouble understanding her on the phone?

   B: Who, Alicia? Not at all. She always speaks _____.
   (clearly / me / understand)

8. **A:** Could you please turn on the air conditioner?

   B: The air conditioner? It's not _____ the air conditioner!
   (hot / need)

9. **A:** You're not drinking your tea. What's wrong with it?

   B: Nothing. It's just still _____.
   (hot / me / drink)

10. **A:** How does Dan like his new phone?

    B: He likes it, and it's _____.
    (easy / him / program)

EXERCISE 5: Editing

Read the text messages. There are eight mistakes in the use of the infinitive of purpose and infinitives after adjectives. The first mistake is already corrected. Find and correct seven more. Check spelling too!

MESSAGES

to remind
ANDREA (4:45 PM): Did you call Sara ~~for reminding~~ her about dinner tomorrow night?

ME (4:50 PM): It's to early to call now. Don't worry. I set my alarm in order no to forget.

ANDREA (5:30 PM): Will you be home enough early to help me with dinner?

ME (5:45 PM): Not sure. I have to stop at the hardware store too buy some more paint for the kitchen.

ANDREA (6:00 PM): Don't we still have paint?

ME (6:05 PM): Yes. But I want to make sure we have enough paint to finishes the job. It'll be a major improvement.

ANDREA (6:10 PM): OK. Would it be too hard to you to make another stop on the way home? I need some butter and eggs for baking the cake for tomorrow night. ☺

ME (6:15 PM): No problem. See you soon. XOXOX

SEND   MENU

EXERCISE 6: Personal Writing

Imagine you just got a new smart phone. What do you use it for? How do you like it? Write a paragraph. Use infinitives and some of the words from the box (or your own ideas).

convenient	expensive	good	(not) too
easy	fun	(not) enough	small

EXAMPLE: *I just got a new phone. I love it. It's small enough to fit inside my pocket and I use it to do many things besides talk. I use it . . .*

_____

_____

_____

_____

_____

_____

_____

_____

_____

_____

_____

_____

Read the notice about a support-group meeting for people who are afraid of flying.
Complete the sentences with the correct form—gerund or infinitive—of the verbs in
parentheses.

Stuck on the ground? Don't wait! Get help now!

Are you afraid of _____ *flying* _____? Stop _____ in fear!
              1. (fly)   **2. (live)**

_____ is the safest form of transportation, but many people are too anxious
    3. (fly)

_____ on a plane.
    4. (get)

Do *you* avoid _____ because you're afraid to leave the ground? Would you
                  5. (fly)

like _____ your fear?
    6. (get over)

Don't let your fear prevent you from _____ all the things that you want
                          7. (do)

_____. You deserve _____ a life free of fear. So, don't put it off.
    8. (do)   **9. (live)**

Decide _____ something about your problem NOW. Come to our monthly
        10. (do)

support-group meetings.

The next meeting is at 7:00 P.M., Tuesday, March 3 at the Community Center. We look

forward to _____ you there.
    11. (see)

And don't forget _____ our website at www.flyaway.com for some helpful
           12. (visit)

tips on _____ yourself off the ground!
    13. (get)

EXERCISE 2: Gerund or Infinitive

These conversations take place at a support-group meeting for people who are afraid of flying. Complete the summary statements about the people. Use the correct verbs or expressions from the box and the gerund or infinitive form of the verbs in parentheses.

afford	be tired of	~~enjoy~~	intend	quit	remember
agree	believe in	forget	offer	refuse	stop

1. **JASON:** Have you ever been to one of these support-group meetings before?

   AMBER: Yes. I like meeting people with the same problem. You get a lot of useful tips.

   SUMMARY: Amber _____*enjoys meeting*_____ people with the same problem.
   (meet)

2. **ANDREA:** Why did you start coming to these meetings?

   HANK: My fear of flying prevents me from doing too many things. It's very discouraging, and I finally want to do something about it.

   SUMMARY: Hank _____ afraid of flying.
   (be)

3. **DYLAN:** Would you like a cup of coffee?

   SYLVIE: No, thanks. I gave up coffee. It makes me too anxious.

   SUMMARY: Sylvie _____ coffee.
   (drink)

4. **CARYN:** I think these meetings are really helpful. You can learn a lot when you talk to other people about your problems.

   PAULO: I agree.

   SUMMARY: Caryn _____ to other people about her problems.
   (talk)

5. **MARY:** Did you bring the travel guide?

   SARA: Oh, no. I left it at work.

   SUMMARY: Sara _____ the travel guide.
   (bring)

6. **AMANDA:** Did you tell Amy about tonight's meeting?

   JOSHUA: No, *you* told Amy about the meeting. I heard you do it.

   AMANDA: Really? Are you sure?

   SUMMARY: Amanda doesn't _____ Amy about the meeting.
   (tell)

7. **Tyler:** You're late. I was getting worried.

    Emily: I'm sorry. On the way over here, I noticed that I was almost out of gas. So I went to fill up the tank.

    summary: Emily _____ gas.
                         (get)

8. **Katie:** I know your parents live in California. How do you get there?

    Mike: I take the train. It's a long trip, and I lose much too much time.

    summary: Mike can't _____ the time.
                         (lose)

9. **Camille:** I was afraid to come to the meeting tonight.

    Vilma: Well, I just *won't* live in fear.

    summary: Vilma _____ in fear.
                         (live)

10. **Erin:** Have you made your flight reservations yet?

    Luis: Not yet. But I'm definitely going to do it.

    summary: Luis _____ a reservation.
                         (make)

11. **Rachel:** Do you think you could help us organize the next meeting?

    Justin: Sure. Just give me a task to do and I'll be glad to help.

    Rachel: We don't have a date yet, but I'll let you know.

    summary: Justin _____ with the next meeting.
                         (help)

12. **Axel:** Would you like a ride home?

    Joanna: Thanks. That would be great.

    summary: Axel _____ Joanna home.
                         (drive)

EXERCISE 3: Gerund or Infinitive

Rewrite the sentences. If the sentence uses the gerund, rewrite it with the infinitive. If the sentence uses the infinitive, rewrite it with the gerund.

1. It's important to talk about your problems.

    Talking about your problems is important.

2. Going to a support group is helpful.

    It's helpful to go to a support group.

(continued on next page)

3. Working together is useful.

_____

4. It's smart to be careful.

_____

5. It's not good to be anxious all the time.

_____

6. Flying isn't dangerous.

_____

7. Doing relaxation exercises is a good idea.

_____

8. Traveling is wonderful.

_____

EXERCISE 4: Editing

Read Hank's post to a fear of flying forum. There are ten mistakes in the use of gerunds and infinitives. The first mistake is already corrected. Find and correct nine more.

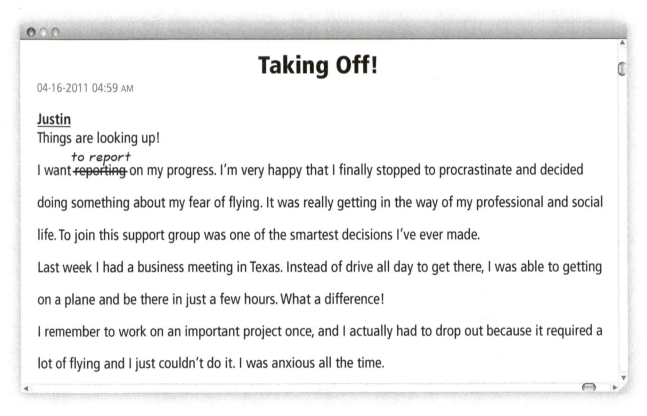

Taking Off!

04-16-2011 04:59 AM

Justin
Things are looking up!

I want ~~reporting~~ _to report_ on my progress. I'm very happy that I finally stopped to procrastinate and decided doing something about my fear of flying. It was really getting in the way of my professional and social life. To join this support group was one of the smartest decisions I've ever made.

Last week I had a business meeting in Texas. Instead of drive all day to get there, I was able to getting on a plane and be there in just a few hours. What a difference!

I remember to work on an important project once, and I actually had to drop out because it required a lot of flying and I just couldn't do it. I was anxious all the time.

My fear was beginning to hurt my friendships too. I was dating a woman I liked a lot and we were supposed to go on a trip. I canceled at the last minute because it required to take a plane.

Now I'm looking forward to do a lot of traveling. I know fear of flying is a universal problem, but it doesn't have to be mine! It's a big world out there, and I plan on enjoy it.

EXERCISE 5: Personal Writing

Write a paragraph about a situation that makes you feel anxious or afraid. What do you do when you feel that way? Use some of the phrases from the box with gerunds or infinitives.

I always try . . .	I keep . . .	I try to remember . . .
I avoid . . .	I never quit . . .	It's important . . .
I imagine myself . . .	I often pretend . . .	Sometimes I can't help . . .

EXAMPLE: *I always get nervous before speaking in front of a group of people. As a result, I try to avoid getting into situations where I need to give a speech. When I can't avoid doing it, I . . .*

_____

_____

_____

_____

_____

_____

_____

_____

_____

_____

UNIT 27 Reflexive and Reciprocal Pronouns

EXERCISE 1: Reflexive Pronouns

Write the reflexive pronouns.

1. I _____ *myself* _____

2. my grandfather _____

3. the class _____

4. my aunt _____

5. you _____ OR _____

6. people _____

7. life _____

8. we _____

EXERCISE 2: Reflexive or Reciprocal Pronouns

Circle the correct pronouns to complete the sentences.

1. Anna and Jim phone each other / themselves every weekend.

2. They have worked with each other / themselves for five years.

3. Anna herself / himself has been with the same company for ten years.

4. It's a nice place. All of the employees consider one another / themselves lucky to be there.

5. They respect each other / each other's opinions.

6. The boss herself / itself is very nice.

7. She tells her employees, "Don't push themselves / yourselves too hard!"

8. Anna enjoys the job herself / itself, but she especially likes her co-workers.

9. My brother and I are considering applying for jobs there myself / ourselves.

10. We talk to each other / ourselves about it when we jog together.

EXERCISE 3: Reflexive or Reciprocal Pronouns

Complete the conversations. Use reflexive or reciprocal pronouns.

1. **A:** What was Marianna's reaction when she lost her job?

   B: At first she was shocked. Then she told _____ *herself* _____ it's a chance to find

   a better job.

2. **A:** What do you do to maintain your relationship with the people you used to work with?

   B: We all live in different places now, but we call and email _____.

3. **A:** How does Miguel like his new job?

   B: Well, the job _____ isn't that interesting, but he really likes the

   people he works with.

4. **A:** So, you finally met Ina!

   B: Yes. I didn't realize that we had so much in common. We really enjoyed talking to

   _____.

5. **A:** Excuse me? I didn't hear what you just said. Could you please repeat it?

   B: Oh, it was nothing. I was just talking to _____! I do that

   from time to time.

6. **A:** Gina! Ricardo! Good to see you both. Come in and help _____

   to some food and drinks.

   B AND C: Thanks! We will. It looks great.

7. **A:** What happened to Frank's face?

   B: Oh, he cut _____ when he was shaving. It looks worse than it is.

8. **A:** You know, giving a party is a lot of work. Maybe we should think about this a little more.

   B: You're right. We need to ask _____ if we really have the time now.

9. **A:** How did you learn to play the guitar? Did you teach _____?

   B: No. A friend taught me.

10. **A:** Who are those two women over there?

    B: Oh, that's Olga and Marta. They just introduced _____ to me.

EXERCISE 4: Verbs with Reflexive or Reciprocal Pronouns

Gina had a party. Read each conversation and complete the summary. Use the correct form of the verbs in parentheses with an appropriate reflexive or reciprocal pronoun.

1. **JOYCE:** This party is a lot of fun.

   HANK: I've never danced with so any people in my life!

   SUMMARY: Joyce and Hank _____ *are enjoying themselves* _____.
   (enjoy)

2. **RON:** We were late because you forgot the address.

   MIA: It's not my fault. You never gave me the slip of paper!

   SUMMARY: Ron and Mia _____.
   (criticize)

3. **GINA:** I'm so glad you could come. There are food and drinks on that table over there.

   Why don't you take a plate and get some?

   CHEN: Thanks. I will. It all looks delicious.

   SUMMARY: Chen _____.
   (help)

4. **AMY:** OK, Amy. Now don't be shy. Go over and talk to that guy over there.

   TIM: Come on, Tim. You can do it. She's looking in your direction. Just go on over.

   SUMMARY: Amy and Tim _____.
   (talk)

5. **AMY:** Hi. I'm Amy.

   TIM: Hi. I'm Tim.

   SUMMARY: Amy and Tim _____.
   (introduce)

6. **AMY:** So, how do you know Gina?

   TIM: Oh, Gina and I were in the same class. What about you?

   SUMMARY: Amy and Tim _____.
   (talk)

7. **PAT:** Did you come with Doug?

   LAURA: No. Doug couldn't make it, but he let me use his car.

   SUMMARY: Laura _____.
   (drive)

8.   **LIZ:** I'm sorry to hear about your job, Hank.

    HANK: It was my fault. I realize that I didn't take it seriously enough, but I've learned my

    lesson. It won't happen again.

    SUMMARY: Hank _____.
                             (blame)

9.   **CARA:** You know, I'm really glad we finally met.

    LIZ: Me too. I feel like we've known each other a long time.

    SUMMARY: Cara and Liz _____ company.
                             (enjoy)

10.   **LIZ:** It was a wonderful party. Thanks for inviting me.

    GINA: Thanks for coming. And thank you for the lovely flowers.

    SUMMARY: Liz and Gina _____.
                             (thank)

EXERCISE 5: Editing

Read Liz's journal entry. There are eleven mistakes in the use of reflexive and reciprocal pronouns. The first mistake is already corrected. Find and correct ten more.

April 25

               myself

I really enjoyed ~~me~~ at Gina's party! Hank was there, and we talked to ourselves

quite a bit. He's a little depressed about losing his job. The job himself wasn't that great,

but the loss of income has really impacted his life. He's disappointed in himself. He thinks

it's all his own fault, and he blames him for the whole thing. Hank introduced myself to

several of his friends. I spoke a lot to this one woman, Cara. We have a lot of things in

common, and after just an hour, we felt like we had known each other's forever. Cara

himself is a computer programmer, just like me.

    At first I was nervous about going to the party alone. I sometimes feel a little

uncomfortable when I'm in a social situation by oneself. But this time was different.

Before I went, I kept telling myself to relax. My roommate too kept telling myself, "Don't

be so hard on you! Just have fun!" That's what I advised Hank to do too. Before we left

the party, Hank and I promised us to keep in touch. I hope to see him again soon.

EXERCISE 6: Personal Writing

Imagine you went to a party last weekend. Who did you go with? What did you do there? Who did you meet? What did you talk about? Did you have a good time? Write a paragraph about the party. Use some of the phrases from the box with reflexive or reciprocal pronouns.

dance	enjoy	introduce	see
drive	help	know	talk

EXAMPLE: *Last Friday night I went to a party by myself. I didn't know anyone there, but I introduced myself to some people. I met a very interesting . . .*

_____

_____

_____

_____

_____

_____

_____

_____

_____

_____

_____

EXERCISE 1: Particles

Complete the phrasal verbs with particles from the box. You will use some particles more than once.

| back | down | in | off | on | out | over | up |

Phrasal Verb   **Definition**

1. call _____off_____   *cancel*

2. call _____   *return a phone call*

3. come _____   *enter*

4. figure _____   *solve*

5. fill _____   *complete*

6. get _____   *return*

7. give _____   *quit*

8. go _____   *continue*

9. grow _____   *become an adult*

10. help _____   *assist*

11. look _____   *be careful*

12. point _____   *indicate*

13. take _____   *get control of*

14. take _____   *remove*

15. think _____   *consider*

16. turn _____   *reject*

17. turn _____   *start a machine*

18. work _____   *exercise*

EXERCISE 2: Phrasal Verbs

Complete the handout for Professor Cho's class. Use the correct phrasal verbs from the box.

do over	help out	look up	~~pick up~~	talk over
hand in	look over	pick out	set up	write up

Science 101   Instructions for Writing the Term Paper   **Prof. Cho**

1. _____*Pick up*_____ a list of topics from the science department secretary.

2. _____ a topic that interests you. (If you are having problems choosing a topic,
   I'll be glad to _____ you _____.)

3. Go online. Use the Internet to _____ information on your chosen topic.

4. _____ an appointment with me to _____ your topic.

5. _____ your first draft.

6. _____ it _____ carefully. Check for accuracy of facts, spelling,
   and grammar errors.

7. _____ your report _____ if necessary.

8. _____ it _____ by May 28.

EXERCISE 3: Phrasal Verbs and Object Pronouns

Complete the conversations between roommates. Use phrasal verbs and pronouns.

1. **A:** I haven't picked up the list of topics for our science paper yet.

   B: No problem. I'll _____*pick it up*_____ for you. I'm going to the science

   office this afternoon.

2. **A:** Hey, guys. We've really got to clean up the kitchen. It's a mess.

   B: It's my turn to _____. I'll do it after dinner.

3. **A:** Did you remember to call your mom back?

   B: Oops! I'll _____ tonight.

4. **A:** Hey, can you turn down that music? I'm trying to concentrate.

   B: Sorry. I'll _____ right away.

5. A: It's after 9:00. Do you think we should wake John up?

   B: Don't _____. He said he wanted to sleep late.

6. A: Professor Cho turned down my science topic.

   B: Really? Why did she _____?

7. A: When do we have to hand in our reports?

   B: We have to _____ by Friday.

8. A: I wanted to drop off my report this afternoon, but I'm not going to have time.

   B: I can _____ for you. I have an appointment with

   Professor Cho at noon.

EXERCISE 4: Word Order

Professor Cho made a list of things to do with her class. Unscramble the words to make sentences. In some cases, more than one answer is possible.

1. the homework problems / back / give

   Give back the homework problems. OR *Give the homework problems back.*

2. out / common mistakes / point

   _____

3. them / over / talk

   _____

4. a new problem / out / pick

   _____

5. it / out / work / with the class

   _____

6. up / the results / write

   _____

7. go / to the next unit / on

   _____

8. up / the final exam questions / make

   _____

(continued on next page)

9. them / out / hand

_____

10. study groups / up / set

_____

11. out / them / help

_____

12. Friday's class / off / call

_____

EXERCISE 5: Editing

Read the student's email. There are eleven mistakes in the use of phrasal verbs. The first mistake is already corrected. Find and correct ten more. A particle in the wrong place counts as one mistake.

Hi, Katy!

How are things going? I'm already into the second month of the spring semester, and I've
                                                                                                          _up_
got a lot of work to do. For science class, I have to write a term paper. The professor made ~~over~~

a list of possible topics. After looking over them, I think I've picked one out. I'm going to write

about chimpanzees and animal intelligence. I've already looked some information about them

online up. I found up some very interesting facts.

Did you know that their hands look very much like their feet,

and that they have fingernails and toenails? Their thumbs and big

toes are "opposable." This makes it easy for them to pick things

out with both their fingers and toes. Their arms are longer than

their legs. This helps out them too, because they can reach fruit

growing on thin branches that would not otherwise support their weight. Adult males weigh

between 90 and 115 pounds, and they are about 4 feet high when they stand out.

Like humans, chimpanzees are very social. They travel in groups called "communities."

Mothers bring out their chimps, who stay with them until about the age of seven. Even after the

chimps grow up, there is still a lot of contact with other chimpanzees.

I could go on, but I need to stop writing now so I can clean out my room (it's a mess!) a little before going to bed. It's late, and I have to get early up tomorrow morning for my 9:00 class.

Please let me know how you are. Or call me. I'm often out, but if you leave a message, I'll call back you as soon as I can. It would be great to speak to you.

Best,

Tony

EXERCISE 6: Personal Writing

How did you find out about this school? Write a paragraph about your experience choosing the school and signing up for class. Use some of the phrasal verbs from the box.

call up	find out	look up	talk over
figure out	help out	pick up	think over
fill out	look over	sign up	write down

EXAMPLE: *I found out about this school from my neighbor. She's been a student here for several years, and she helped me fill out the forms . . .*

_____

_____

_____

_____

_____

_____

_____

_____

_____

_____

_____

PART IX

MORE MODALS AND SIMILAR EXPRESSIONS

UNIT 29 Necessity: *Have (got) to, Must, Don't have to, Must not, Can't*

EXERCISE 1: Affirmative and Negative Statements with *Must*

Read the driving rules. Complete the sentences with **must** *or* **must not** *and the verbs from the box.*

change	drive	~~have~~	leave	pass	stop	turn on
drink	forget	know	obey	sit	talk	wear

1. In almost all countries, you _____*must have*_____ a valid license in order to drive.

2. You _____ a road test to get a license.

3. You _____ to carry your license with you at all times when you drive. Don't forget it!

4. You _____ all traffic signs. They are there for a reason!

5. When you see a stop sign, you _____. Don't just slow down.

6. You _____ faster than the maximum speed limit.

7. You _____ lanes without signaling.

8. When it's dark, you _____ your headlights.

9. You _____ the scene of an accident. Wait until the police arrive.

10. In most countries, the driver and passengers _____ seat belts.

11. In some places, you _____ on a cell phone unless you have a headset. Make sure you know the local laws.

12. Small children _____ in a special safety seat.

13. Alcohol and driving don't mix. You _____ absolutely never _____ and drive.

14. Driving regulations differ from country to country. You _____ the rules before you take to the road in a foreign country!

Read about driving rules in different countries. Complete the statements with the correct form of **have to** or **don't have to** and the verbs in parentheses.

	Minimum driving age	Maximum speed limit on major highway	Side of road	Seat belt law	Warning triangle	First-aid kit
Canada	16	62 mph/ 100 kmh*	right	driver and passengers	no	no
Germany	18	none	right	driver and passengers	yes (1)	yes
Indonesia	17	62 mph/ 100 kmh	left	driver and front seat passenger	no	no
Italy	18	81 mph/ 130 kmh	right	driver and passengers	yes (1)	recommended
Mexico	18	68 mph/ 110 kmh	right	driver and passengers	no	no
Turkey	18	74 mph/ 120 kmh	right	driver and passengers	yes (2)	yes

*depends on the part of the country

1. You _____*have to be*_____ eighteen years old to drive in most of the countries.
   (be)

2. You _____ eighteen in Canada and Indonesia.
   (be)

3. You _____ slower than 81 mph (130 kmh) in Turkey.
   (drive)

4. A driver _____ slower than 81 mph (130 kmh) in Germany.
   (go)

5. In Indonesia, drivers _____ on the left side of the road.
   (drive)

6. In Mexico, both the driver and passengers _____ a seat belt.
   (wear)

7. In Indonesia, backseat passengers _____ a seat belt.
   (use)

8. Turkish cars _____ two warning triangles to use in case they are
   (carry)
   involved in an accident.

9. In Germany, cars _____ two warning triangles.
   (have)

10. In Germany and Turkey, you _____ a first-aid kit in your car.
    (keep)

11. In Italy, you _____ one in your car.
    (have)

EXERCISE 3: Contrast: *Must not* or *Don't have to*

Look at the chart in Exercise 2 on page 169. Complete the statements with **must not** *or the correct form of* **don't have to.**

1. If you are under the age of eighteen, you _____ *must not* _____ drive in most of the countries listed in the chart.

2. You _____ be eighteen to drive in Canada.

3. You _____ obey a speed limit on major German highways.

4. In Turkey, you _____ drive on the left side of the road.

5. In Mexico, drivers _____ carry a warning triangle.

6. In Indonesia, passengers in the back seat _____ wear seat belts.

7. You _____ drive without a first-aid kit in Germany and Turkey.

8. You _____ have a first-aid kit in Italy.

EXERCISE 4: Statements, Questions, and Short Answers with *Have to*

Complete the conversations with short answers or the correct form of **have to** *(present, past, future, or present perfect) and the verbs in parentheses.*

1. **A:** Did you pass your road test the first time you took it?

   B: No. I _____ *had to take* _____ it two more times before I passed! What a hassle!
   (take)

2. **A:** _____ we _____ for gas?
   (stop)

   B: _____. The tank's almost empty.

3. **A:** How many times _____ you _____ public
   (use)

   transportation <u>since</u> you moved here?

   B: Only once. When my car broke down.

4. **A:** _____ you _____ late yesterday?
   (work)

   B: _____. Luckily, I finished on time.

5. **A:** Are you thinking of buying a new car?

   B: Not yet. But in a couple of years, I _____ another one.
   (get)

6. **A:** Why didn't you come to the meeting last night?

   B: I _____ my uncle to the airport.
   (drive)

7. A: My wife got a speeding ticket last week. She was really annoyed. She was only going five miles above the speed limit.

B: Really? How much _____ she _____?
(pay)

A: It was more than $100. They've gotten very strict about enforcing speed limits.

8. A: _____ your son ever _____ for a traffic violation?
(pay)

B: _____. He's a very careful driver.

9. A: _____ I _____ a new license when I move?
(get)

B: _____. You can only use an out-of-state license for 10 days.

10. A: Do you have car insurance?

B: Of course. Everyone in this country _____ car insurance.
(have)

11. A: How often _____ you _____ your car inspected in your state?
(get)

B: Every two years.

EXERCISE 5: Contrast: *Must, Must not, Have to,* and *Can't*

Read the online test questions about road signs in the United States. Fill in the circle next to the correct answer.

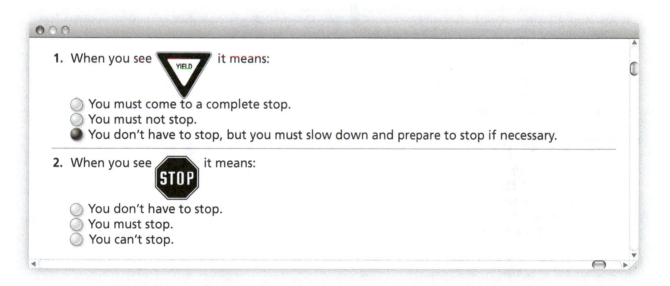

1. When you see [YIELD] it means:

   ○ You must come to a complete stop.
   ○ You must not stop.
   ● You don't have to stop, but you must slow down and prepare to stop if necessary.

2. When you see [STOP] it means:

   ○ You don't have to stop.
   ○ You must stop.
   ○ You can't stop.

(continued on next page)

3. When you see **SPEED LIMIT 50** it means:

- ○ You must drive 50 miles per hour.
- ○ You must not drive faster than 50 miles per hour.
- ○ You don't have to drive more than 50 miles per hour.

4. When you see **NO TURN ON RED** it means:

- ○ You have to turn when the light is red.
- ○ You don't have to turn when the light is red.
- ○ You must not turn when the light is red.

5. When you see **DO NOT ENTER** it means:

- ○ You must not enter.
- ○ You don't have to enter.
- ○ You must enter.

6. When you see **DO NOT PASS** it means:

- ○ You don't have to pass another car.
- ○ You can't pass another car.
- ○ You have to pass another car.

7. When you see **ONE WAY** it means:

- ○ You must drive in the direction of the arrow.
- ○ You must not drive in the direction of the arrow.
- ○ You don't have to drive in the direction of the arrow.

8. When you see **MAXIMUM SPEED 65 MINIMUM SPEED 45** it means:

- ○ You have to drive 45 miles per hour or slower.
- ○ You can't drive 70 miles per hour.
- ○ You don't have to drive 70 miles per hour.

9. When you see **NO LEFT TURN** it means:

- ○ You must turn left.
- ○ You can't turn left.
- ○ You don't have to turn right.

10. When you see **Ⓟ 8:30AM TO 5:30PM** it means:

- ○ You can't park at 5:00 A.M.
- ○ You must not park at 7:00 P.M.
- ○ You don't have to move your car at 6:00 P.M.

EXERCISE 6: Editing

Read the email. There are eight mistakes in expressing necessity. The first mistake is already corrected. Find and correct seven more.

Hi, Jason!

Sorry I haven't written before, but there are so many things I've ~~must~~ *had to* do since we moved

to California. For one, I have to taking a driving test. My brother is lucky. He must not

take one because he got a license when he was a student here. And you really have to

drive if you live here—it's very hard to get around without a car! So, I've been studying

the Driver Handbook, and I've found some pretty interesting—and sometimes

strange—things:

  You can't smoke when a minor (that's someone under the age of eighteen) is in the car.

  You can use a cell phone, but you has got to use one with a hands-free device.

  You must no "dump or abandon animals on a highway." (I can't imagine anyone doing

  this, can you?) If you do, you will probably must pay a fine of $1,000 or go to jail for six

  months, or both!

Did you must take a road test when you moved to Italy?

I've got go now. Let me hear from you!

R.

Write a paragraph about a time you moved. What did you have to do? What didn't you have to do? Use some of ideas from the box and your own ideas.

buy furniture	learn to drive
find a place to live	make new friends
learn a new language	paint

EXAMPLE: *Moving is difficult. There are so many things you have to do. When I first came to this country, I stayed with my aunt and uncle. That was good because I didn't have to find an apartment right away. There were, however, many other things that I had to do. I had to . . .*

_____

_____

_____

_____

_____

_____

_____

_____

_____

_____

_____

EXERCISE 1: Affirmative and Negative Statements with *Be supposed to*

Today, in some countries, when people get married, the groom's family often shares the expenses, and older couples often pay for their own weddings. However, some people are still traditional. Read the chart and complete the sentences with a form of **be supposed to.**

TRADITIONAL WEDDING ETIQUETTE: WHO DOES WHAT	
Role of the Bride's Family	**Role of the Groom's Family**
send invitations pay for food supply flowers pay for the groom's ring provide music	pay for the bride's ring give a rehearsal dinner[1] pay for the honeymoon provide beverages

[1] **rehearsal dinner:** a dinner that usually takes place the night before the wedding ceremony, attended by the bride, the groom, people who will be part of the ceremony, and often out-of-town guests

1. The groom's family _____ *isn't supposed to send* _____ the invitations.

2. The bride's family _____ the invitations.

3. The bride's parents _____ the music.

4. The groom's parents _____ the music.

5. The groom's family _____ the groom's ring.

6. The groom's family _____ the bride's ring.

7. The bride's parents _____ the honeymoon.

8. The groom's family _____ the honeymoon.

9. The bride's parents _____ the rehearsal dinner.

10. The groom's parents _____ the rehearsal dinner.

11. The groom's family _____ the flowers.

12. The bride's family _____ the food.

13. The groom's family _____ the beverages.

Erica Nelson is getting married. She completed this change-of-address form, but she made eight mistakes. Find the mistakes and write sentences with **was supposed to** *and* **wasn't supposed to.** *Include the number of the item that has the mistake.*

U.S. Postal Sevice CHANGE OF ADDRESS ORDER	Customer Instructions: Complete Items 1 thru 9, Except Item 8, please PRINT all information including address on face of card.	OFFICIAL USE ONLY

1. Change of address for *(Check one)*   ☑ Individual   ☑ Entire Family   ☐ Business

Zone/Route Id No.

2. Start Date   Month Day Year `3 0 0 6 9 5`   3. If TEMPORARY address, print date to discontinue forwarding   Month Day Year

Date Entered on Form 3982   M M D D Y Y

4. Print Last Name or Name of Business *(If more than one use, use separate Change of Address Order Form for each)*   `E R I C A`

Expiration Date   M M D D Y Y

5. Print First Name of Head of Household (include Jr., Sr., etc.). Leave Blank if the Change of Address Order is for a business.   `N e l s o n`

Clerk/Carrier Endorsements

6. Print OLD mailing address, number and street *(if Puerto Rico, include urbanization zone)*   `2 6   M A P L E   R O A D`

Apt./Suite No. `4 A`   P.O. Box No.   R.R/HCR No.   Rural Box/HCR Box No.

City `B O S T O N`   State `M A`   Zip Code `–`

7. Print NEW Mailing address, number and street *(if Puerto Rico, include urbanization zone)*   `2 9 8 7   C O S B Y   A V E`

Apt./Suite No.   P.O. Box No.   R.R/HCR No.   Rural Box/HCR Box No.

City `A M H E R S T`   State   Zip Code `–`

8. Signature *(See conditions on reverse)*   *Erica Nelson*

OFFICIAL USE ONLY

9. Date Signed   Month Day Year

OFFICIAL USE ONLY

Verification Endorsement

PS Form 3575, June 1991   ☆ U.S.G.P.O. 1992-309-315

1. Item ___1___   *She was supposed to check one box.*

OR

She wasn't supposed to check two boxes.

2. Item _____

3. Item _____

4. Item _____

5. Item _____

6. Item _____

7. Item _____

8. Item _____

EXERCISE 3: Questions and Answers with *Be supposed to*

Erica and her new husband are on their honeymoon. Complete the conversations. Use the words from the box and **be supposed to.** *Use short answers when necessary.*

~~arrive~~	call	get	leave	shake
be	do	land	rain	tip

1. **ERICA:** What time ___are___ we ___supposed to arrive___ in Bermuda?

   ADAM: Well, the plane _____ at 10:30, but it looks like we're going to be late.

2. **ERICA:** What time _____ we _____ to the hotel?

   ADAM: Check-in time is 12:00.

3. **ERICA:** _____ we _____ if we're going to be late?

   ADAM: _____. We'd better call as soon as we land.

4. **ADAM:** How much _____ we _____ the person who carries our bags for us?

   ERICA: I think it's $1.00 a bag.

5. **ADAM:** _____ the hotel restaurant _____ good?

   ERICA: _____. The travel agent suggested that we go somewhere else for dinner.

6. **ERICA:** What _____ we _____ with our keys when we leave the hotel? Can we take them with us?

   ADAM: We _____ them at the front desk.

7. **ERICA:** _____ it _____ today?

   ADAM: No. _____. But look at those clouds. I think we'd better take an umbrella just in case.

8. **ERICA:** Can you hand me that bottle of sunblock?

   ADAM: Sure. _____ you _____ the bottle before you use it?

   ERICA: I don't know. What do the instructions say?

EXERCISE 4: Affirmative and Negative Statements with *Was / Were going to*

Read about Erica and Adam's plans. Write two sentences for each item. Use **was(n't)** *or* **were(n't) going to.**

1. Erica planned to be a doctor, but she became a lawyer instead.

   a. _Erica was going to be a doctor._

   b. _She wasn't going to become a lawyer._

2. Adam didn't plan to get married. He planned to stay single.

   a. _____

   b. _____

3. Erica and Adam planned to get married in June, but they got married in September.

   a. _____

   b. _____

4. They didn't plan to have a big wedding. They planned to have a small one.

   a. _____

   b. _____

5. Erica's sister was supposed to select the flowers, but Adam's assistant did it instead.

   a. _____

   b. _____

6. They wanted a short ceremony, but it was long.

   a. _____

   b. _____

7. They planned to live in Boston, but they moved to Amherst.

   a. _____

   b. _____

8. Adam didn't plan to change jobs. He planned to keep his old one.

   a. _____

   b. _____

EXERCISE 5: Editing

Read Erica's postcard. There are six mistakes in the use of **be supposed to** and **was** or **were going to.** The first mistake is already corrected. Find and correct five more.

Greetings from Bermuda

Here we are in beautiful Bermuda. It's sunny, 80°, and it ~~will~~ 's supposed to get even warmer

later today.

    I'm so glad we decided to come here for our honeymoon. At first, we was going to go to

London, but we decided we really needed a relaxing beach vacation instead. The hotel is very

nice. We were supposed to get a standard double room, but when they found out we were on

our honeymoon, they upgraded us to a suite with an ocean view. Tonight we're eating at Chez

Marcel's. It supposes to be one of the best restaurants on the island.

    Gotta go now. I suppose to meet Adam in a few minutes. He's going to join me at the

beach, but decided to play some tennis instead.

    Thanks for offering to pick us up at the airport. We're supposed to arriving at 5:30 P.M.,

but check with the airport before to see if there are any delays. See you soon!

Love,

Erica

EXERCISE 6: Personal Writing

Everyone makes plans, but plans often change. Write a paragraph about your own changed plans. Use some of the phrases from the box.

> I was supposed to . . . , but . . .
>
> I wasn't supposed to . . . , but . . .
>
> I was going to . . . , but . . .
>
> I wasn't going to . . . , but . . .

EXAMPLE: *Three years ago I was supposed to move to California, but my plans changed. My father got a job in Texas, and so my family and I moved here instead. We were supposed to . . .*

_____

_____

_____

_____

_____

_____

_____

_____

_____

_____

_____

EXERCISE 1: Affirmative and Negative Statements

Read Lauren's journal entry. Complete the sentences with the words in parentheses.
Choose between affirmative and negative.

Thursday, July 3

I was supposed to go to the beach tomorrow, but the weather forecast says it

_____ might rain _____. I'm not really sure what I'll do if it rains. I think I
    1. (might / rain)

_____ shopping at the mall instead. It's a holiday weekend,
    2. (may / go)

so there _____ some good sales. I really need some new
    3. (could / be)

clothes. I _____ find a dress for John's party. Maybe I'll
    4. (might / be able to)

call Julie. She _____ to go with me. That would be great.
    5. (might / want)

She always knows the latest clothing trends.

    On second thought, shopping _____ such a good idea.
        6. (may / be)

The stores will probably be really crowded. I _____ to a
        7. (could / go)

movie instead. There's a Spanish film at the local movie theater, but I'm a little afraid

that I _____ enough of it. My Spanish really isn't that
    8. (might / understand)

good. Maybe I'll call Eric and ask him if he wants to take a drive to see Aunt Marla

and Uncle Phil. He _____ to go, though, because he doesn't
        9. (might / want)

like driving in the rain. It's crazy how much the weather affects people's plans. Oh,

well. I _____ home and read a good book. That
    10. (could / stay)

_____ the best thing to do.
    11. (might / be)

EXERCISE 2: Contrast: *Be going to* or *Might*

*Read the conversations. Use **be going to** or **might** and the verbs from the box to complete the summary sentences.*

buy	go	rain	see	work
call	have	read	~~visit~~	write

1. **LAUREN:** Hello, Julie? This is Lauren. Do you want to go to the mall with me?

   JULIE: I don't know. I'm thinking about going to my parents'.

   SUMMARY: Julie _____ *might visit* _____ her parents.

2. **JULIE:** What are you looking for at the mall?

   LAUREN: I need to get a new dress for John's party.

   JULIE: Good luck! I hope you find something.

   SUMMARY: Lauren _____ a new dress.

3. **LAUREN:** Do you think we'll get some rain?

   CARL: Definitely. Look at those clouds.

   SUMMARY: Carl thinks it _____.

4. **LAUREN:** What are you doing today?

   CARL: I have tickets for a play.

   SUMMARY: Carl _____ a play.

5. **LAUREN:** What are you doing this weekend?

   KAYLA: I'm not sure. I'm thinking about taking a drive to the country.

   SUMMARY: Kayla _____ for a ride.

6. **LAUREN:** Say, Eric. Do you want to see Aunt Marla and Uncle Phil tomorrow?

   ERIC: I can't. I have to go into the office this weekend—even though it's a holiday.

   SUMMARY: Eric _____ this weekend.

7. **LAUREN:** How about dinner Saturday night?

   ERIC: That's an idea. Can I call and let you know tomorrow?

   LAUREN: Sure.

   SUMMARY: Lauren and Eric _____ dinner together.

8. **LAUREN:** Hi, Aunt Marla. How are you?

  MARLA: Lauren! How are you? It's good to hear your voice. Listen, we just started dinner. Can I call you back?

  LAUREN: Sure.

  MARLA: OK. I'll speak to you later.

  SUMMARY: Marla _____ Lauren later.

9. **MARLA:** Hi. It's Aunt Marla. Sorry about before. What are you doing home on a holiday weekend? Why aren't you out?

  LAUREN: I'm tired. I just want to stay home with a good book.

  SUMMARY: Lauren _____ a book.

10. **MARLA:** Do you have any other plans?

  LAUREN: Maybe I'll catch up on some of my email.

  SUMMARY: Lauren _____ some email.

EXERCISE 3: Editing

Read Lauren's email. There are five mistakes in the use of modals to express future possibility. The first mistake is already corrected. Find and correct four more.

Hi, Rachel,

How are you? It's the Fourth of July, and it's raining really hard. They say it could ~~cleared~~ *clear* up later. Then again, it ~~could~~ *might* not. You never know with the weather.

Do you remember my brother, Eric? He says hi. He might ~~has~~ *have* dinner with me on Saturday night. We may go to a new Mexican restaurant that just opened in the mall.

I definitely ~~might~~ *will* take some vacation time next month. Perhaps we could do something together. It might not be fun to do some traveling. What do you think? Let me know.

Lauren

EXERCISE 4: Personal Writing

A. *Make a short "To Do" list for next weekend. Put a question mark (?) next to the things you aren't sure you'll do.*

To Do

1.
2.
3.
4.
5.
6.
7.
8.

B. *Now write a paragraph about what you* **are going to do** *and what you* **might do.**

EXAMPLE: *I have a lot of plans for next weekend, but I know I won't be able to do everything.
I'm definitely going to watch the football game with Tom and Lisa, but I might not
have time to finish painting the kitchen . . .*

UNIT 32 Conclusions: *Must, Have (got) to, May, Might, Could, Can't*

EXERCISE 1: Affirmative and Negative Statements with *Must*

Read the facts. Complete the conclusions with **must** *or* **must not***.*

1. Jack is wearing a gold wedding band on his ring finger.

   CONCLUSION: He _____*must be*_____ married.
   (be)

2. You have been calling Alicia since 8:00 P.M., but no one answers the phone.

   CONCLUSION: She _____ home.
   (be)

3. Christa got 98 percent on her math test.

   CONCLUSION: Her parents _____ proud of her.
   (feel)

4. Carlos works from 9:00 to 5:00 and then attends night school.

   CONCLUSION: He _____ a lot of free time.
   (have)

5. Martin works as a mechanic in Al's Automobile Shop.

   CONCLUSION: He _____ a lot about cars.
   (know)

6. Monica owns two houses and four cars.

   CONCLUSION: She _____ a lot of money.
   (have)

7. Mr. Cantor always asks me to repeat what I say.

   CONCLUSION: He _____ well.
   (hear)

8. Chen got only four hours of sleep last night.

   CONCLUSION: He _____ very tired today.
   (feel)

9. Tyrone has been at R & L, Inc. for more than 20 years.

   CONCLUSION: He _____ a good position there.
   (have)

10. This job advertisement doesn't mention the salary.

    CONCLUSION: That's not a good sign. It _____ very good!
    (be)

11. Carmen was born in Mexico and moved to the United States when she was ten.

    CONCLUSION: She _____ Spanish.
    (speak)

(continued on next page)

12. Mindy never gets good grades.

  CONCLUSION: She _____ enough.
  (study)

13. Dan just bought a bottle of aspirin and four boxes of tissues.

  CONCLUSION: He _____ a cold.
  (have)

14. Ana and Giorgio didn't have any of the steak.

  CONCLUSION: They _____ meat.
  (eat)

15. Detective Menendez solves a lot of crimes.

  CONCLUSION: His methods _____ very effective.
  (be)

EXERCISE 2: Contrast: *Must* or *May / Might / Could*

Read the conversations. Circle the appropriate words.

1. A: Someone broke into the Petersons' house.

   B: That's terrible! What did they take?

   A: All of Mrs. Peterson's jewelry.

   B: Oh, no. She could / **must** feel awful.

   A: Is she home now? I'd like to call her.

   B: I don't know. She might / must be home. She sometimes gets home by 6:00.

2. A: Do the Petersons have insurance?

   B: Oh, they could / must. Mr. Peterson works at an insurance company.

3. A: Have you checked our burglar alarm lately?

   B: Yes. And I just put in a new battery.

   A: Good. So it must / might be OK.

4. A: Do you remember that guy we saw outside the Petersons' home last week?

   B: Yes. Why? Do you think he might / must be the burglar?

   A: I don't know. I guess he must / could be the burglar. He looked a little suspicious.

   B: Maybe we should tell the police about him.

   A: Maybe.

5. A: Someone's at the door.

   B: Who <u>could / must</u> it be?

   A: I don't know.

   B: Detective Menendez wanted to ask us some questions about the burglary.

   A: Oh. It <u>must / could</u> be him. We're not expecting anybody else.

6. A: How old do you think Detective Menendez is?

   B: Well, he's been a detective for ten years. So he <u>must / might</u> be at least thirty-five.

   A: You're right. He <u>couldn't / might not</u> be much younger than thirty-five. He probably started out as a police officer and became a detective in his mid-twenties.

   B: He looks a lot younger, though.

EXERCISE 3: Short Answers with *Must* or *May, Might, Could*

Write a short answer to each question. Use **must, may, might,** *or* **could** *and include* **be** *where necessary.*

1. A: Is Ron a reporter?

   B: _____*He might be*_____. He always carries a notepad and asks a lot of questions.

2. A: Does Marta speak Spanish?

   B: _____. She lived in Spain for four years.

3. A: Do the Taylors have a lot of money?

   B: _____. They're always taking very expensive vacations.

4. A: Is Ricardo married?

   B: _____. He wears a wedding ring.

5. A: Does Anna know Meng?

   B: _____. They both work for the same company, but it's very big.

6. A: Is your phone out of order?

   B: _____. It hasn't rung once today, and John always calls me by this time.

7. A: Is that online encyclopedia any good?

   B: _____. It's *very* popular.

(continued on next page)

8. A: Are Marcia and Scott married?

    B: _____. They both have the same last name, but it's possible that

    they're brother and sister.

9. A: Does Glenda drive?

    B: _____. She owns a car.

10. A: Is Oscar an only child?

    B: _____. I don't know. He's never mentioned a brother or sister.

11. A: Are the Hendersons away?

    B: _____. I haven't seen them for a week, and there are no lights on

    in their apartment.

EXERCISE 4: Contrast: *Might, Must, Could, Can't, Couldn't, Might not*

Read the description of a burglary suspect and look at the four pictures. Complete the conversation with the correct words and the names of the men in the pictures.

21-year-old white male

short, curly blond hair

no scars or other

distinguishing features

Allen

Bob

Chet

Dave

DETECTIVE: Please look at these four photos. It's possible that one of these men

    _____*could*_____ be the man we're looking for. Take your time.
        1. (must / could)

WITNESS 1: Hmmm. What do you think? _____ it be this man?
                                   2. (could / must)

WITNESS 2: It _____ be _____. He has a scar
                     3. (can't / must)   **4. (Name)**

        on his face. What about _____? He has short blond hair and
                                            5. (Name)

        looks like he's twenty-one.

WITNESS 1: I'm not sure. It _____ be. But it _____
                           6. (could / must)   **7. (might / must)**

        also be _____. He also has blond hair and looks twenty-one.
                       8. (Name)

WITNESS 2: But he has long hair.

WITNESS 1: The photo _____ be old. Maybe he cut it.
                          9. (could / couldn't)

WITNESS 2: That's true. Well, it definitely _____ be
                                 10. (couldn't / might not)

        _____. He looks too old. Maybe we could look at some
                  11. (Name)

        more photos.

EXERCISE 5: Editing

Read the man's email. There are five mistakes in the use of modals to express conclusions.
The first mistake is already corrected. Find and correct four more.

                                      must

Just got home. It's really cold outside. The temperature ~~could~~ be below freezing because the

walkway is all covered with ice. What a day! We went down to the police station to look at

photos. I was amazed. They must having hundreds of photos. They kept showing us more and

more. We kept looking, but it was difficult to be sure. After all, we only saw the burglar for a few

seconds. They've got to have other witnesses besides us! There were a lot of people at the mall

that day. We may not be the only ones who got a look at the burglar! That's the one thing I'm

certain of! In spite of our uncertainty with the photos, the detective was very patient. I guess he

must be used to witnesses like us. Nevertheless, it have to be frustrating for him. I know the

police may really want to catch this guy!

Read the description of the burglar in Exercise 4 on page 188. Look at the pictures. Is one of them the burglar? What's your opinion? Write a paragraph. Use **could be, might be, may be, couldn't be,** *and* **can't be.** *Give reasons for your opinions.*

Ed

Frank

George

EXAMPLE: *It isn't always easy to identify someone. Is one of these men the burglar? It couldn't be . . . because . . .*

_____

_____

_____

_____

_____

_____

_____

_____

_____

_____

_____

WORKBOOK ANSWER KEY

In this answer key, where the contracted form is given, the full form is often also correct, and where the full form is given, the contracted form is often also correct.

UNIT 17 (pages 101–105)

EXERCISE 1

A

Tut's Tomb: An Egyptian Time Capsule

Tutankhamun, better known as King Tut, became king of ancient Egypt when he was only nine years old. He died before his nineteenth birthday around 1323 B.C.E., and was mostly forgotten. Thousands of years later, British archeologist Howard Carter searched for his tomb. In 1922, after searching for many years, he finally found it near the Nile River, across from the modern Egyptian city of Luxor. Inside he discovered thousands of items buried along with the young king. Among the many treasures were:

- furniture—including couches and chairs
- jewelry—including bracelets and necklaces
- clothing—including gloves, scarves, and shoes
- musical instruments
- chariots
- vases and jars
- pots made of clay (they probably once contained money)
- games and toys (Tut played with them as a child)
- food and wine
- gold

Tut's tomb is a time capsule. It gives us a picture of how Egyptian kings lived more than 3000 years ago, how they died, and what they expected to need in their lives after death.

Since his discovery, Tut has not been resting in peace. He and his treasures have traveled to exhibitions around the world, where millions of visitors have been able to view some of the wonders of his ancient civilization.

B

Proper nouns: Tutankhamun, King, Egypt, Howard Carter, Nile, Luxor

Common count nouns: *Answers will vary.*
Some possibilities: time capsule, years, birthday, archeologist, river, city, items, king, treasures, couches, chairs, bracelets, necklaces, gloves, scarves, shoes, instruments, chariots, vases, jars, pots, games, toys, child, picture, lives, discovery, exhibitions, world, visitors, wonders, civilization

Common non-count nouns: jewelry, clothing, clay, money, food, wine, gold, death, peace

EXERCISE 2

2. country lies
3. people live
4. Cairo has
5. Cotton is
6. Rice grows
7. tourists visit
8. Ramadan takes place
9. shops and restaurants close
10. weather is
11. clothing is
12. sunhats are OR a sunhat is

EXERCISE 3

2. many	12. a few
3. several	13. some
4. a few	14. a lot of
5. many	15. some
6. a lot of	16. some
7. much	17. some
8. many	18. many
9. much	19. Many
10. some	20. many
11. a lot of	21. a lot of

EXERCISE 4

I can't tell you how much we enjoyed our trip to ~~egypt~~ *Egypt*. We just returned ~~few~~ *a few* days ago. What an amazing country! There are so ~~much~~ *many* things to see and do. My only complaint ~~are~~ *is* that we didn't have enough time! But, we'll be back!
Hannes Koch, Germany

We saw a lot of tombs and pyramids on our recent trip, but the best were the three Giza pyramids. ~~It is~~ *They are* huge! And, I was surprised to learn, they are located right at the edge of the city of Cairo. Because of this, there is a lot of traffic getting there (and back). There were also a lot *of* tourists. The day we were there it was very hot. If you go, you should know that there are ~~a few~~ *few* places to get anything to drink, so I REALLY recommend that you bring ~~any~~ *some* water with you. Oh, and if you want to see the inside of a pyramid, you need a special ticket, and they only sell a ~~little~~ *few* tickets each day. Get there early if you want one!

Vilma Ortiz, USA

The food ~~are~~ *is* great in Egypt! We went to some wonderful ~~Restaurants~~ *restaurants*. We found out about one place near our hotel that doesn't have ~~much~~ *many* tourists. Mostly local people ~~eats~~ *eat* there and everyone was really friendly. I particularly enjoyed the "meze" (a variety of appetizers). You choose a ~~little~~ *few* different plates before you order your main dish. Delicious!

Jim Cook, England

There are many beautiful ~~beach~~ *beaches* in Alexandria. A lot of them are private or connected to hotels, but there are also public ones, so be sure to bring a bathing suit if you visit that part of Egypt. The water ~~were~~ *was* warm—like being in a bathtub!

Aki Kato, Japan

EXERCISE 5

Answers will vary.

UNIT 18 (pages 106–110)

EXERCISE 1

1. the, the	**7.** Ø, Ø, the, Ø
2. the	**8.** the, an, the
3. the	**9.** an, a
4. the, the	**10.** Ø, Ø
5. a, The, the	**11.** some, a, the, the
6. the	**12.** the, a, The

EXERCISE 2

2. a	**13.** The
3. the	**14.** the
4. A	**15.** the
5. a	**16.** the
6. —	**17.** the
7. —	**18.** the
8. a	**19.** an
9. —	**20.** —
10. The	**21.** a
11. —	**22.** —
12. a	**23.** the

EXERCISE 3

2. a	**15.** an
3. a	**16.** the
4. the	**17.** the
5. the	**18.** The
6. the	**19.** a
7. the	**20.** the
8. the	**21.** the
9. the	**22.** the
10. The	**23.** The
11. the	**24.** the
12. a	**25.** the
13. the	**26.** —
14. the	**27.** the

EXERCISE 4

A fox is ~~the~~ *a* member of the dog family. It looks like ~~the~~ *a* small, thin dog with ~~an~~ *a* bushy tail, a long nose, and pointed ears. You can find ~~the~~ foxes in most parts of ~~a~~ *the* world. ~~Animal~~ *The animal* moves very fast, and it is ~~the~~ *a* very good hunter. It eats mostly mice, but it also eats ~~the~~ birds, insects, rabbits, and fruit.

Unfortunately, ~~a~~ people hunt foxes for their beautiful fur. They also hunt them for another reason. The fox is ~~a~~ *an* intelligent, clever animal, and this makes it hard to catch. As a result, ~~the~~ hunters find it exciting to try to catch one. It is also because of its cleverness that a fox often appears in fables, such as ~~a~~ *the* fable we just read in class.

EXERCISE 5

Answers will vary.

UNIT 19 (pages 111–116)

EXERCISE 1

2. nice	**11.** sudden
3. fast	**12.** peacefully
4. well	**13.** angrily
5. dangerous	**14.** convenient
6. beautifully	**15.** badly
7. hard	**16.** thoughtful
8. safely	**17.** hungry
9. ideal	**18.** extremely
10. happy	

EXERCISE 2

2. Good news travels fast
3. It has five large rooms
4. it's in a very large building

5. it's very sunny
6. We're really satisfied with it
7. It's not too bad
8. It seems pretty quiet
9. he speaks very loudly
10. He doesn't hear well
11. Was it a hard decision
12. we had to decide quickly
13. I have to leave now
14. Good luck with your new apartment

EXERCISE 3

2. hard
3. really
4. well
5. nice
6. extremely
7. comfortable
8. cold
9. pretty
10. friendly
11. safe
12. really
13. important
14. late
15. completely
16. empty
17. good
18. easily
19. near
20. frequently
21. nice
22. convenient
23. wonderful
24. completely
25. new
26. really
27. happy
28. happy

EXERCISE 4

2. disturbed
3. entertaining
4. disgusted
5. inspiring
6. paralyzed
7. moving
8. moved
9. frightening
10. disturbed
11. touching
12. astonishing
13. frightening
14. bored
15. disappointed
16. touching
17. exciting
18. entertaining
19. bored

EXERCISE 5

2. tall handsome Italian actor
3. large new TV
4. delicious fresh mushroom pizza
5. comfortable black leather sofa
6. nice small student apartment
7. quiet residential neighborhood
8. enjoyable, relaxing evening
9. small comfortable, affordable apartment OR small affordable, comfortable apartment

EXERCISE 6

Charming

~~Charmingly~~, one-bedroom apartment in a

peaceful residential

~~residential peaceful~~ neighborhood.

Conveniently

~~Convenient~~ located near shopping, transportation, entertainment, and more.

- affordable rent
- all-new appliances

  beautiful antique French
- ~~French antique beautiful~~ desk
- friendly neighbors

  safe
- clean and ~~safely~~ neighborhood

  close
- ~~closely~~ to park
- quiet building

This great apartment is ideal for students, and

immediately

it's ~~immediate~~ available. Call 444–HOME for an

disappointed

appointment. You won't be ~~disappointing~~! But act

fast   *amazing apartment*

~~fastly~~! This ~~apartment amazing~~ won't last long.

EXERCISE 7

Answers will vary.

UNIT 20 (pages 117–123)

EXERCISE 1

2. worse
3. bigger
4. more careful
5. cheaper
6. more comfortable
7. more crowded
8. more delicious
9. earlier
10. more expensive
11. farther OR further
12. fresher
13. better
14. hotter
15. noisier
16. more relaxed
17. more terrible
18. more traditional
19. more varied
20. wetter

EXERCISE 2

2. not as large as
3. just as big as
4. just as expensive as
5. not as varied as
6. not as long as
7. not as convenient as
8. not as late as
9. not as nice as
10. just as good as
11. not as good as
12. just as clean as

EXERCISE 3

2. earlier
3. more comfortable
4. healthier than
5. more interesting than, better than, fresher
6. taller than
7. worse, quieter (OR more quiet) than, more relaxed
8. later than
9. faster
10. easier

EXERCISE 4

2. Y . . . cheaper than . . . X
3. Y . . . larger than . . . X
4. X . . . smaller than . . . Y
5. Y . . . heavier than . . . X
6. X . . . lighter than . . . Y
7. X . . . more efficient than . . . Y
8. Y . . . more effective than . . . X
9. Y . . . faster than . . . X
10. X . . . slower than . . . Y
11. X . . . noisier than . . . Y
12. Y . . . quieter (OR more quiet) than . . . X
13. Y . . . better than . . . X
14. X . . . worse than . . . Y

EXERCISE 5

2. cheaper and cheaper OR less and less expensive
3. better and better
4. bigger and bigger
5. more and more varied
6. more and more popular
7. less and less healthy
8. heavier and heavier

EXERCISE 6

2. The fresher the ingredients, the better the food.
3. The more popular the restaurant, the longer the lines.
4. The more enjoyable the meal, the more satisfied the customers.
5. The bigger the selection, the happier the customers.
6. The later in the day, the more tired the servers (get).
7. The more crowded the restaurant, the slower the service.
8. The better the service, the higher the tip.

EXERCISE 7

I just got home from the Pizza Palace. Wow! The
pizza there just keeps getting ~~good~~ *better* and better. And,
of course, the better the food, the ~~more long~~ *longer* the
lines, and the ~~crowdeder~~ *more crowded* the restaurant! But I don't
really mind. It's totally worth it. Tonight Ana and I
shared a pizza with spinach, mushrooms, and
~~fresher~~ *fresh* tomatoes. It was much more interesting ~~as~~ *than* a
traditional pizza with just tomato sauce and cheese.
It's also healthier ~~than~~. And the ingredients were as
fresh ~~than~~ *as* you can find anywhere in the city. (Although
I usually think the pizza at Joe's Pizzeria is fresher.)

It was so large that we couldn't finish it, so I brought
the rest home. Actually, I'm getting hungry again
just thinking about it. I think I'll pop a slice into the
microwave and warm it up. It will probably taste
almost as ~~better~~ *good* as it tasted at the Pizza Palace!

EXERCISE 8

Answers will vary.

UNIT 21 (pages 124–129)

EXERCISE 1

2. the worst
3. the biggest
4. the cutest
5. the most dynamic
6. the most expensive
7. the farthest OR the furthest
8. the funniest
9. the best
10. the happiest OR the most happy
11. the hottest
12. the most important
13. the most intelligent
14. the most interesting
15. the lowest
16. the nicest
17. the noisiest OR the most noisy
18. the most practical
19. the warmest
20. the most wonderful

EXERCISE 2

2. Mexico City . . . the newest
3. New York City . . . the longest
4. Toronto . . . the shortest
5. The busiest . . . New York City
6. Toronto . . . the lowest
7. Toronto . . . the most expensive (OR Mexico City . . . the least expensive)
8. the cheapest . . . Mexico City

EXERCISE 3

2. the newest
3. the most beautiful
4. the easiest
5. the biggest
6. the least comfortable
7. the fastest
8. the coolest
9. the hottest
10. the most convenient
11. the most interesting
12. the least dangerous
13. the most historic
14. the most crowded
15. The most efficient
16. the most dangerous
17. the least expensive
18. the quietest OR the most quiet

EXERCISE 4

Greetings from Mexico City! With its mixture of the
old and the new, this is one of the ~~interestingest~~ *most interesting*
cities I've ever visited. The people are among the
~~friendlier~~ *friendliest* OR *most friendly* in the world, and they have been very
patient with my attempts to speak their language.
Spanish is definitely one of ~~a~~ *the* most beautiful
languages, and I really want to take lessons when
I get home. This has been the ~~most hot~~ *hottest* summer in
years, and I'm looking forward to going to the beach
next week. The air pollution is also the ~~baddest~~ *worst* I've
experienced, so I'll be glad to be out of the city. By
the way, we definitely did not need to rent a car. The
~~most fast~~ *fastest* and ~~convenientest~~ *most convenient* way to get around is by
subway.

EXERCISE 5

Answers will vary.

UNIT 22 (pages 130–135)

EXERCISE 1

2. worse — the worst
3. more beautifully — the most beautifully
4. more carefully — the most carefully
5. more consistently — the most consistently
6. more dangerously — the most dangerously
7. earlier — the earliest
8. more effectively — the most effectively
9. farther OR further — the farthest OR the furthest
10. faster — the fastest
11. more frequently — the most frequently
12. harder — the hardest
13. more intensely — the most intensely
14. less — the least
15. longer — the longest
16. more — the most
17. more quickly — the most quickly
18. more slowly — the most slowly
19. sooner — the soonest
20. better — the best

EXERCISE 2

2. ran as fast as
3. jumped as high as
4. didn't jump as high as
5. didn't throw the discus as far as
6. threw the discus as far as
7. didn't do as well as
8. didn't compete as successfully as

EXERCISE 3

2. harder than
3. more slowly than OR slower than
4. faster
5. more consistently
6. more aggressively than
7. worse than
8. better
9. more effectively
10. more intensely
11. (more) frequently

Winning Team: Jamil, Randy, Carlos
Losing Team: Alex, Rick, Larry, Elvin

EXERCISE 4

2. E . . . the most slowly OR the slowest, more slowly OR slower than
3. higher than . . . B
4. E . . . the highest
5. farther than . . . E
6. E . . . the farthest
7. E . . . the best
8. E . . . the worst . . . better than

EXERCISE 5

2. She's running more and more frequently.
3. He's throwing the ball farther and farther.
4. She's shooting more and more accurately.
5. He's jumping higher and higher.
6. He's running more and more slowly OR slower and slower.
7. They're skating (OR dancing) more and more gracefully. OR They're scoring higher and higher.
8. They're practicing longer and longer.
9. He's driving more and more dangerously.
10. They're feeling worse and worse.

EXERCISE 6

I just completed my run. I'm running much longer
~~that~~ *than* before.
Today I ran for 30 minutes without getting out of
breath. I'm glad I decided to run ~~more slow~~ *more slowly* OR *slower*. The
more slowly I run, the ~~farthest~~ *farther* I can go. I'm really
seeing progress.
Because I'm enjoying it, I run more and more
~~frequent~~ *frequently*. And the more often I do it, the longer and
farther I can go. I really believe that running
helps me feel better more ~~quick~~ *quickly* than other forms of
exercise. I'm even sleeping better than before!
I'm thinking about running in the next marathon. I

as fast as OR *faster than*

may not run ~~as fast than~~ younger runners, but I

longer

think I can run ~~long~~ and farther. We'll see!

EXERCISE 7

Answers will vary.

EXERCISE 1

2. going
3. meeting
4. Sitting
5. running
6. lifting
7. doing
8. taking
9. Exercising
10. wasting

EXERCISE 2

2. Dancing
3. lifting weights
4. walking (OR playing tennis) . . . playing tennis (OR walking)
5. swimming
6. lifting weights
7. walking (OR riding a bike) . . . riding a bike (OR walking)
8. Doing sit-ups
9. swimming
10. lifting weights (OR doing sit-ups), doing sit-ups (OR lifting weights)
11. running
12. playing tennis
13. Riding a bike
14. lifting weights

EXERCISE 3

2. dislikes doing OR doesn't enjoy doing
3. enjoys dancing
4. mind teaching
5. kept practicing
6. denied (OR denies) stepping OR didn't admit (OR doesn't admit) stepping
7. considering taking
8. regrets not beginning
9. suggests going OR suggested going
10. admits feeling OR admitted feeling
11. banned smoking OR doesn't permit smoking
12. permits smoking

EXERCISE 4

2. to having
3. in quitting
4. about passing
5. on staying, finishing
6. of staying, of getting
7. in having
8. of permitting, to smoking

EXERCISE 5

banning

I'm in favor of ~~ban~~ smoking in all public places. I

smoking

think ~~to smoke~~ should be illegal in parks and at beaches.

of

I approve ~~to~~ having free programs that help people

smoking

quit ~~to smoke~~.

Advertising

~~To advertise~~ cigarettes in newspapers and magazines is alright.

is

Smoking cigarettes ~~are~~ a private decision, and the government should not make laws against it.

lighting

If people enjoy ~~to light~~ up a cigarette, that is their right.

EXERCISE 6

Answers will vary.

EXERCISE 1

2. want to see
3. refuses to go
4. threatened to end
5. hesitate (OR am hesitating) to take
6. seems to be
7. attempted to create
8. intend to stay
9. needs to speak
10. will agree to go

EXERCISE 2

2. to do the dishes.
   him to do the dishes.
3. her to buy some milk.
   to buy some milk.
4. him to drive her to her aunt's.
   to drive her to her aunt's.
5. him to have dinner at her place Friday night.
   to have dinner at her place Friday night.
6. him to give her his answer tomorrow.
   to give her his answer tomorrow.
7. to cut his hair.
   her to cut his hair.
8. him to be home at 7:00.
   to get home at 8:00.
9. her to call him before she left the office.
   to call him before she left the office.
10. to see a movie Friday night.
    her to pick one out.
11. to ask his boss for a raise.
    him to do it.

12. to get some more stamps.
　to stop at the post office on the way home.

EXERCISE 3

　　　　　　　　　　　　　　　to hear
Annie answered my letter. I didn't expect ~~hearing~~
back from her so soon! She agrees that seeing a
counselor is a good idea for John and me, but she
　　　us
advised ~~we~~ to go to counseling separately at first.
That idea never even occurred to me, but I think that
it's a really excellent suggestion. I don't know if John
　　　　to go
will agree ~~going~~, but I'm definitely going to ask him
to think about it when I see him on Saturday. I
attempted to introduce the topic last night, but he
　　　　not to
pretended ~~to not~~ hear me. (He's been doing that a lot
lately. He seems to think if he ignores a question, I'll
just forget about it!) I won't give up, though. I'm
　　　　　　　　him
going to try to persuade ~~he~~ to go. I have no idea how
to find a counselor, so if he agrees to go, I may ask
　　to
Annie ^ recommend some in our area. Obviously, I
　　to find
want ~~finding~~ someone really good.
I still believe in us as a couple. Our relationship
　　　　　　　　　　　　　to
deserves to have a chance, and I'm prepared ^ give it
　　　　to feel
one. But I want John ~~feels~~ the same way. Afterall, it
takes more than one person to make a relationship. I
really need to know that he's 100 percent committed
to the relationship. I can be patient, but I can't afford
to wait
~~waiting~~ forever.

EXERCISE 4

Answers will vary.

UNIT 25 (pages 147–152)

EXERCISE 1

2. You can use cell phones and smart phones to
take pictures.
3. You can use smart phones to search online.
4. You can use smart phones to send email.
5. You can use cell phones, smart phones, and
PDAs to connect to the Internet.
6. You can use smart phones and PDAs to create a
"To Do" list.
7. You can use cell phones, smart phones, and
PDAs to store addresses.
8. You can use smart phones to play music.
9. You can use smart phones to translate words.

EXERCISE 2

3. He uses most of his salary (in order) to pay his
college tuition.
4. He really wants an MP3 player (in order) to
download music from the Internet.
5. He's going to wait for a sale in order not to pay
the full price.
6. A lot of people came into the store today (in
order) to look at the new multipurpose devices.
7. They like talking to Ned (in order) to get
information about the devices.
8. Someone bought a GPS in order not to get lost.
9. Another person bought a tiny camcorder (in
order) to bring it on vacation.
10. She used her credit card in order not to pay
right away.
11. Ned showed her how to use the camcorder (in
order) to do a lot of things.
12. She'll use it as a camera (in order) to take
videos.

EXERCISE 3

2. to have　　　　　**5.** to leave
3. to pay　　　　　**6.** to take
4. to eat　　　　　**7.** to find

EXERCISE 4

2. good enough for me to do
3. too late to go
4. fast enough to leave
5. too tired to stay
6. too late to call
7. clearly enough for me to understand
8. hot enough to need
9. too hot for me to drink
10. easy enough for him to program

EXERCISE 5

　　　　　　　　　　　　　　　　to remind
ANDREA (4:45 PM): Did you call Sara ~~for reminding~~
　　　　　　　　　　　　her about dinner tomorrow
　　　　　　　　　　　　night?
　　　　　　　　　too
ME (4:50 PM): It's ~~to~~ early to call now. Don't
　　　　　　　　worry. I set my alarm in order
　　　　　　　　not
　　　　　　　　~~no~~ to forget.
　　　　　　　　　　　　　　　early enough
ANDREA (5:30 PM): Will you be home ~~enough early~~
　　　　　　　　　　　　to help me with dinner?
ME (5:45 PM): Not sure. I have to stop at the
　　　　　　　　　　　　　　　to
　　　　　　　　hardware store ~~too~~ buy some
　　　　　　　　more paint for the kitchen.
ANDREA (6:00 PM): Don't we still have paint?

ME **(6:05 PM):** Yes. But I want to make sure we

                                     finish

have enough paint to ~~finishes~~

the job. It'll be a major

improvement.

                                            for

ANDREA **(6:10 PM):** OK. Would it be too hard ~~to~~ you

to make another stop on the

way home? I need some butter

                       to bake

and eggs ~~for baking~~ the cake for

tomorrow night. ☺

ME **(6:15 PM):** No problem. See you soon.

XOXOX

EXERCISE 6

Answers will vary.

UNIT 26 (pages 153–157)

EXERCISE 1

2. living	**8.** to do
3. Flying	**9.** to live
4. to get	**10.** to do
5. flying	**11.** seeing
6. to get over	**12.** to visit
7. doing	**13.** getting

EXERCISE 2

2. is tired of being	**7.** stopped to get
3. quit (OR stopped) drinking	**8.** afford to lose
4. believes in talking	**9.** refuses to live
5. forgot to bring	**10.** intends to make
6. remember telling	**11.** agreed to help
	12. offered to drive

EXERCISE 3

3. It's useful to work together.
4. Being careful is smart.
5. Being anxious all the time isn't good.
6. It isn't dangerous to fly.
7. It's a good idea to do relaxation exercises.
8. It's wonderful to travel.

EXERCISE 4

          to report

I want ~~reporting~~ on my progress. I'm very happy that

          procrastinating   *to do*

I finally stopped ~~to procrastinate~~ and decided ~~doing~~

something about my fear of flying. It was really

getting in the way of my professional and social life.

Joining

~~To join~~ this support group was one of the smartest

decisions I've ever made.

Last week I had a business meeting in Texas. Instead

driving   *get*

of ~~drive~~ all day to get there, I was able to ~~getting~~ on

a plane and be there in just a few hours. What a

difference!

          working

I remember ~~to work~~ on an important project once,

and I actually had to drop out because it required a

lot of flying and I just couldn't do it. I was anxious all

the time.

My fear was beginning to hurt my friendships too.

I was dating a woman I liked a lot and we were

supposed to go on a trip. I canceled at the last

                           taking

minute because it required ~~to take~~ a plane.

                   doing

Now I'm looking forward to ~~do~~ a lot of traveling. I

know fear of flying is a universal problem, but it

doesn't have to be mine! It's a big world out there,

          enjoying

and I plan on ~~enjoy~~ it.

EXERCISE 5

Answers will vary.

UNIT 27 (pages 158–162)

EXERCISE 1

2. himself
3. itself
4. herself
5. yourself, yourselves OR yourselves, yourself
6. themselves
7. itself
8. ourselves

EXERCISE 2

2. each other	**7.** yourselves
3. herself	**8.** itself
4. themselves	**9.** ourselves
5. each other's	**10.** each other
6. herself	

EXERCISE 3

2. one another OR each other
3. itself
4. each other OR one another
5. myself
6. yourselves
7. himself
8. ourselves
9. yourself
10. themselves

EXERCISE 4

2. are criticizing each other OR one another
3. is going to help himself
4. are talking to themselves
5. are introducing themselves
6. are talking to each other
7. drove herself
8. blames OR is blaming himself
9. are enjoying each other's OR one another's
10. are thanking each other OR one another

EXERCISE 5

             myself
I really enjoyed ~~me~~ at Gina's party! Hank was
         each other OR *one another*
there and we talked to ~~ourselves~~ quite a bit. He's a
                          itself
little depressed about losing his job. The job ~~himself~~
wasn't that great, but the loss of income has really
impacted his life. He's disappointed in himself. He
                       himself
thinks it's all his own fault, and he blames ~~him~~ for
               me
the whole thing. Hank introduced ~~myself~~ to several
of his friends. I spoke a lot to this one woman, Cara.
We have a lot of things in common, and after just an
            each other
hour, we felt like we had known ~~each other's~~ forever.
       herself
forever. Cara ~~himself~~ is a computer programmer, just
like me.

    At first I was nervous about going to the party
alone. I sometimes feel a little uncomfortable when
               myself
I'm in a social situation by ~~oneself~~. But this time was
different. Before I went, I kept telling myself to relax.
               me
My roommate too kept telling ~~myself~~, "Don't be so
     yourself
hard on ~~you~~! Just have fun!" That's what I advised
Hank to do too. Before we left the party, Hank and
each other OR *one another* OR ∅
I promised ~~us~~ to keep in touch. I hope to see him
again soon.

EXERCISE 6

Answers will vary.

UNIT 28 (pages 163–167)

EXERCISE 1

2. back	7. up	12. out	17. on
3. in	8. on	13. over	18. out
4. out	9. up	14. off	
5. out	10. out	15. over	
6. back	11. out	16. down	

EXERCISE 2

2. Pick out, help . . . out	6. Look . . . over
3. look up	7. Do . . . over
4. Set up, talk over	8. Hand . . . in
5. Write up	

EXERCISE 3

2. clean it up	6. turn it down
3. call her back	7. hand them in
4. turn it down	8. drop it off
5. wake him up	

EXERCISE 4

2. Point out common mistakes. OR Point common mistakes out.
3. Talk them over.
4. Pick out a new problem. OR Pick a new problem out.
5. Work it out with the class.
6. Write up the results. OR Write the results up.
7. Go on to the next unit.
8. Make up the final exam questions. OR Make the final exam questions up.
9. Hand them out.
10. Set up study groups. OR Set study groups up.
11. Help them out.
12. Call off Friday's class. OR Call Friday's class off.

EXERCISE 5

    How are things going? I'm already into the
second month of the spring semester, and I've got a
lot of work to do. For science class, I have to write
                                   up
a term paper. The professor made ~~over~~ a list of
                       them over
possible topics. After looking ~~over them~~, I think
I've picked one out. I'm going to write about
chimpanzees and animal intelligence. I've already
                 up
looked some information about them online ~~up~~. I
       out
found ~~up~~ some very interesting facts.

    Did you know that their hands look very much
like their feet, and that they have fingernails and
toenails? Their thumbs and big toes are "opposable."
This makes it easy
                      up
for them to pick things ~~out~~ with both their fingers
and toes. Their arms are longer than their legs. This
               them out
helps ~~out them~~ too, because they can reach fruit
growing on thin branches that would not otherwise
support their weight. Adult males weigh between 90
and 115 pounds, and they are about 4 feet high when
            up
they stand ~~out~~.

Like humans, chimpanzees are very social. They travel in groups called "communities." Mothers bring *up* ~~out~~ their chimps, who stay with them until about the age of seven. Even after the chimps grow up, there is still a lot of contact with other chimpanzees.

I could go on, but I need to stop writing now so I can clean *up* ~~out~~ my room (it's a mess!) a little before going to bed. It's late, and I have to get *up early* ~~early up~~ tomorrow morning for my 9:00 class.

Please let me know how you are. Or call me. I'm often out, but if you leave a message, I'll call *you back* ~~back you~~ as soon as I can. It would be great to speak to you.

EXERCISE 6

Answers will vary.

UNIT 29 (pages 168–174)

EXERCISE 1

2. must pass
3. must not forget
4. must obey
5. must stop
6. must not drive
7. must not change
8. must turn on
9. must not leave
10. must wear
11. must not talk
12. must sit
13. must . . . drink
14. must know

EXERCISE 2

2. don't have to be
3. have to drive
4. doesn't have to drive
5. have to drive
6. have to wear
7. have to use
8. have to carry
9. don't have to have
10. have to keep
11. don't have to keep

EXERCISE 3

2. don't have to
3. don't have to
4. must not
5. don't have to
6. don't have to
7. must not
8. don't have to

EXERCISE 4

2. **A:** Do . . . have to stop
   B: Yes, we do.
3. **A:** have . . . had to use
4. **A:** Did . . . have to work
   B: No, I didn't.
5. **B:** 'll have to get OR 'm going to have to get
6. **B:** had to drive
7. **B:** did . . . have to pay
8. **A:** Has . . . had to pay
   B: No, he hasn't.

9. **A:** Will (OR Do) . . . have to get OR
   Am . . . going to have to get
   B: Yes, you will. OR you do. OR you are.
10. **B:** has to have
11. **A:** do . . . have to get

EXERCISE 5

2. You must stop
3. You must not drive faster than 50 miles per hour.
4. You must not turn when the light is red.
5. You must not enter.
6. You can't pass another car.
7. You must drive in the direction of the arrow.
8. You can't drive 70 miles per hour.
9. You can't turn left.
10. You don't have to move your car at 6:00 P.M.

EXERCISE 6

Sorry I haven't written before, but there are so many things I've *had to* ~~must~~ do since we moved to California. For one, I have to *take* ~~taking~~ a driving test. My brother is lucky. He *doesn't have to* ~~must not~~ take one because he got a license when he was a student here. And you really have to drive if you live here—it's very hard to get around without a car! So, I've been studying the Driver Handbook, and I've found some pretty interesting—and sometimes strange—things:

You can't smoke when a minor (that's someone under the age of eighteen) is in the car.

You can use a cell phone, but you *have* ~~has~~ got to use one with a hands-free device.

You must *not* ~~no~~ "dump or abandon animals on a highway." (I can't imagine anyone doing this, can you?) If you do, you will probably *have to* ~~must~~ pay a fine of $1,000 or go to jail for six months, or both!

Did you *have to* ~~must~~ take a road test when you moved to Italy?

I've got ˄*to* go now. Let me hear from you!

EXERCISE 7

Answers will vary.

UNIT 30 (pages 175–180)

EXERCISE 1

2. is supposed to send
3. are supposed to provide
4. aren't supposed to provide
5. isn't supposed to pay for

6. is supposed to pay for
7. aren't supposed to pay for
8. is supposed to pay for
9. aren't supposed to give
10. are supposed to give
11. isn't supposed to supply
12. is supposed to pay for
13. is supposed to provide

EXERCISE 2

2. Item 2: She was supposed to write the month first. OR She wasn't supposed to write the day first.
3. Item 4: She was supposed to print (OR write) her last name. OR She wasn't supposed to print (OR write) her first name.
4. Item 5: She was supposed to print (OR write) her first name. OR She wasn't supposed to print (OR write) her last name.
5. Item 6: She was supposed to write (OR include) her zip code.
6. Item 7: She was supposed to write (OR include) her state and (her) zip code.
7. Item 8: She was supposed to sign her name. OR She wasn't supposed to print her name.
8. Item 9: She was supposed to write the date.

EXERCISE 3

1. is (OR was) supposed to land
2. are . . . supposed to get
3. Are . . . supposed to call
   Yes, we are.
4. are . . . supposed to tip
5. Is . . . supposed to be
   No, it isn't.
6. are . . . supposed to do
   're supposed to leave
7. Is . . . supposed to rain
   No, it isn't.
8. Are . . . supposed to shake

EXERCISE 4

2. a. Adam wasn't going to get married.
   b. He was going to stay single.
3. a. Erica and Adam were going to get married in June.
   b. They weren't going to get married in September.
4. a. They weren't going to have a big wedding.
   b. They were going to have a small one.
5. a. Erica's sister was going to select the flowers.
   b. Adam's assistant wasn't going to do it.
6. a. They were going to have a short ceremony. OR The ceremony was going to be short.
   b. They weren't going to have a long ceremony. OR The ceremony wasn't going to be long.
7. a. They were going to live in Boston.

b. They weren't going to move to Amherst.
8. a. Adam wasn't going to change jobs.
   b. He was going to keep his old one.

EXERCISE 5

Here we are in beautiful Bermuda. It's sunny, 80°, and it ~~will~~ 's supposed to get even warmer later today. I'm so glad we decided to come here for our honeymoon. At first, we ~~was~~ were going to go to London, but we decided we really needed a relaxing beach vacation instead. The hotel is very nice. We were supposed to get a standard double room, but when they found out we were on our honeymoon, they upgraded us to a suite with an ocean view. Tonight we're eating at Chez Marcel's. ~~It supposes~~ It's supposed to be one of the best restaurants on the island. Gotta go now. ~~I suppose~~ I'm supposed to meet Adam in a few minutes. ~~He's~~ He was going to join me at the beach, but decided to play some tennis instead. Thanks for offering to pick us up at the airport. We're supposed to ~~arriving~~ arrive at 5:30 P.M., but check with the airport before to see if there are any delays. See you soon!

EXERCISE 6

Answers will vary.

UNIT 31 (pages 181–184)

EXERCISE 1

2. may go
3. could be
4. might be able to
5. might want
6. may not be
7. could go
8. might not understand
9. might not want
10. could stay
11. might be

EXERCISE 2

2. might buy
3. is going to rain
4. is going to see
5. might go
6. is going to work
7. might have
8. is going to call
9. is going to read
10. might write

EXERCISE 3

How are you? It's the Fourth of July, and it's raining really hard. They say it could ~~cleared~~ clear up later. Then again, it ~~could~~ might OR may not. You never know with the weather.

Do you remember my brother, Eric? He says

hi. He might ~~has~~ _have_ dinner with me on Saturday night. We may go to a new Mexican restaurant that just opened in the mall.

I definitely ~~might take~~ _am going to take_ OR _am taking_ some vacation time next month. Perhaps we could do something together. It might ~~not~~ be fun to do some traveling. What do you think? Let me know.

EXERCISE 4

Answers will vary.

UNIT 32 (pages 185–190)

EXERCISE 1

2. must not be
3. must feel
4. must not have
5. must know
6. must have
7. must not hear
8. must feel
9. must have
10. must not be
11. must speak
12. must not study
13. must have
14. must not eat
15. must be

EXERCISE 2

1. might
2. must
3. must
4. might, could
5. could, must
6. must, couldn't

EXERCISE 3

2. She must
3. They must
4. He must be
5. She might (not) OR may (not) OR could
6. It must be
7. It must be
8. They might be OR may be OR could be
9. She must
10. He might be OR may be OR could be
11. They must be

EXERCISE 4

2. Could
3. can't
4. Bob
5. Chet
6. could
7. might
8. Dave
9. could
10. couldn't
11. Allen

EXERCISE 5

Just got home. It's really cold outside. The

temperature ~~could~~ _must_ be below freezing because the walkway is all covered with ice. What a day! We went down to the police station to look at photos. I was

amazed. They must ~~having~~ _have_ hundreds of photos. They kept showing us more and more. We kept looking, but it was difficult to be sure. After all, we only saw the burglar for a few seconds. They've got to have other witnesses besides us! There were a lot of

people at the mall that day. We ~~may not~~ _can't_ OR _couldn't_ be the only ones who got a look at the burglar! That's the one thing I'm certain of! In spite of our uncertainty with the photos, the detective was very patient. I guess he must be used to witnesses like us. Nevertheless, it

~~have~~ _has_ to be frustrating for him. I know the police ~~may~~ _must_ really want to catch this guy!

EXERCISE 6

Answers will vary.